North Wales Walks & Legends

Showell Styles
with Henry Stilwell

Copyright © Showell Styles, 1972, 2002
Additional text by Henry Stilwell © 2002
First published by Granada, 1972; republished in 1990 by John Jones Cardiff Ltd. This revised edition published by Sigma Leisure in 2002

Published by Sigma Leisure – an imprint of
Sigma Press, 1 South Oak Lane, Wilmslow, Cheshire SK9 6AR, England.

British Library Cataloguing in Publication Data
A CIP record for this book is available from the British Library.

ISBN: 1-85058-792-2

Typesetting and Design by: Sigma Press, Wilmslow, Cheshire.
Editing and additional material by: Graham Beech

Cover design: Sigma Leisure
Maps: sketch maps, Morag Perrott; location map, Eric Jones
Illustrations: Siân Davies

Printed by: MFP Design and Print

Disclaimer: the information in this book is given in good faith and is believed to be correct at the time of publication. No responsibility is accepted by either the author or publisher for errors or omissions, or for any loss or injury howsoever caused. Only you can judge your own fitness, competence and experience. Do not rely solely on sketch maps for navigation: we strongly recommend the use of appropriate Ordnance Survey (or equivalent) maps.

Introduction

This book is for visitors to Wales who want to see the best of its varied scenery and in doing so learn something of its traditions and history. It is for those who are prepared to walk short distances from the car, but who don't want to have to don mountaineering clothes and heavy boots – or leave the children behind. It tells 18 legends of North Wales and helps you to see for yourself where each long-ago happening, historical or imaginary, took place. Most of the walks are short and easy, a few longer to suit the more energetic; but none of them will occupy more than half a day unless you take a picnic along.

For convenience, the stories are placed under area headings. In fact, the areas overlap considerably, and in most cases the walks can be done from any of the centres mentioned, if you have a car. I shall tell you the story of the legend first and then describe in detail how to reach its location. The reference map after this introduction will enable you, by reference to the information at the start of each walk description, to find the whereabouts of the place you are heading for. Those who carry the Ordnance Survey maps will find at the start of every walk the Grid Reference, preceded by the Sheet number of the map required. If you intend to tackle some of the longer walks, you will need the larger scale (1:25,000) OS Explorer or Outdoor Leisure maps; where appropriate, these are mentioned.

When I did the walks myself (in the 1960s) all the paths and routes described were open and public, with no access impediments. Since then, rights of way have been established and the original routes have been adapted by Henry

Stilwell, where necessary, to ensure that you are directed along roads, tracks and paths to which the public have access. The times given for each walk make no allowance for long halts or picnics but are a generous estimate of actual walking time.

As to the legends, they are traditional and a few of them factual – though even these have been embroidered over the years. Several different versions of some of the legends exist, and where this is the case, I've simply picked the one I liked best.

Showell Styles

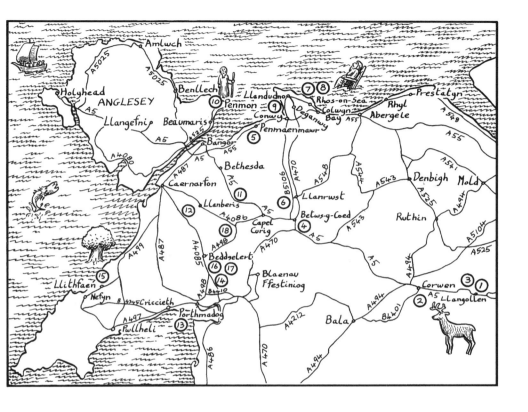

Key to Location Map

1. **World's End:** Nest and her Lovers
2. **Corwen:** The White Hart of Llangar
3. **Llangollen:** Myfanwy of Dinas Brân
4. **Betws-y-Coed:** The Legend of the Afanc
5. **Penmaenmawr:** The Stone Women of Moelfre
6. **Llyn Geirionydd:** Taliesin The Bard
7. **Rhôs-on-Sea:** The End of Maelgwn Gwynedd
8. **Rhôs-on-Sea:** How Prince Madoc Discovered America

9. **Deganwy** and its Castle
10. **Anglesey:** The Isle of St Seiriol
11. **Llyn Idwal:** The Lake that no Bird will Cross
12. **Betws Garmon:** The Farmer Who Caught a Fairy
13. **Borth y Gest:** The Rising of the Lark
14. **Croesor:** Helen's Spring
15. **Llithfaen:** The Accursed Village
16. **Beddgelert:** The Story of Gelert
17. **Beddgelert:** Glyndẁr's Chimney
18. **Snowdon:** King Arthur's Last Battle

Contents

The Vale of Llangollen

1.
World's End: Nest and her Lovers

2.
Corwen: The White Hart of Llangar

3.
Llangollen: Myfanwy of Dinas Brân

1. World's End:
Nest and her Lovers

King Henry I of England was no more restrained in his passions than any other powerful ruler of the 12th century. It made little difference to him that the beautiful Nest, daughter of the Welsh prince Rhys ap Tudor, had been placed in his care as a Royal Ward; he fell in love with Nest and seduced her, and she bore him a son.

In those days, however, there was an accepted way of dealing with such a situation. Nest's baby son was named Duke of Gloucester and King Henry gave Nest in marriage to one of his barons, Gerald de Windsor – whom, it seems, was in love with her himself. Gerald was Earl of Pembroke, and took his new wife with him to South Wales, where the fame of her beauty soon spread far beyond those parts – as far, even, as the kingdoms of Gwynedd and Powys in the north. Though Gerald was a Norman baron and maintained an armed force in Pembroke Castle, he was on terms of slightly uneasy peace with Prince Cadwgan, Welsh ruler of this land of Ceredigion as well as of Powys, and the Earl and Countess lived in peace and happiness for a year. Then came a Christmas when Cadwgan ordained a great Eisteddfod in South Wales, to which everyone of distinction flocked, including the Welsh countess. And with the guests came Cadwgan's daredevil son, Owain.

Now Owain lived in his father's second kingdom of Powys, in a hunting-lodge called Plas Eglwyseg at the head of a secret glen north of the Dee. Here, he had gathered about him a band of reckless fighting-men, with whom he would sally forth by the path he called his war path to hunt, or raid, or harass King Henry's men-at-arms. He was accustomed to take for himself whatever he wanted. And when he came to his father's Eisteddfod and set eyes on the lovely Nest he determined at once to carry her off. That very night he and his men broke into the castle of Pembroke, set it on fire, and dragged Nest from the bed where she was sleeping with her husband. The Earl, naked and unarmed, escaped with his life by way of a drain-pipe. Nest was borne away across the mountains to Owain's retreat at Plas Eglwyseg, where (it appears) she lived quite happily with her captor for some time.

But the mad action of Owain ap Cadwgan brought terrible consequences. King Henry, appealed to by Gerald de Windsor, ordered Prince Cadwgan to restore the stolen countess on pain of losing his kingdoms. Cadwgan's attempts to comply met with flat defiance from his son, who eluded all efforts to capture him; and war broke out through the whole

of Wales. Norman barons aided Cadwgan's Welsh rivals to take Powys from him and others robbed him of much of his southern kingdom. The new rulers of Powys disinherited Owain and at last succeeded in driving him out of his refuge at Plas Eglwyseg, whence he fled to Ireland, leaving Nest homeless. The deserted beauty made her way southward and, after a long and hazardous journey, reached Pembroke Castle, where Earl Gerald – now the most powerful lord in South Wales – took her in his arms and once more established her as his wife and countess.

Then, for a year or more, there was a period of peace. It was broken by the arrival of a raiding force from Ireland, which was opposed by the Earl of Pembroke in alliance with the Welsh. Owain had accompanied the raiders, but now elected to change sides and fight for his native land. In the midst of the battle, Gerald recognised the man who had wronged him fighting on the same side as himself. Changing the direction of his attack, he and his bodyguard fell upon Owain and slew him, thus wiping out, to the satisfaction of the people who counted in those days, the dishonour he had suffered at Owain's hands.

Gerald de Windsor ended his warlike career by dying peacefully in his castle of Carew, but his wife's career was not finished. Though her children were now grown up and married, Nest still had her beauty – and plenty of love to spare. She transferred her affections first to Stephen, Constable of Caernarfon Castle, and then to the Sheriff of Pembroke, presenting each of them with a son. All her children, legitimate or illegitimate, founded great families; and if you are a Fitzgerald, a Carew, a Barry, or a Fitzstephen you are very probably of 'the race of Nesta'.

The Walk
To Plas Eglwyseg and World's End

How to get there: First, find the centre of Llangollen. If arriving from the west, e.g. Betws-y-Coed, enter on the A5 and turn left at the traffic lights into the town centre. The A5 also enters the town from the Chirk direction, the A539 from Ruabon and the A542 from the north). By whatever route you arrived, cross the bridge over the River Dee and turn right then immediately left up Wharf Hill. Cross the canal bridge and go past a school called Ysgol Dinas Brân on your right. The lane climbs gently for a short distance until you turn right, sign-posted to Worlds End. From here, the lane is narrow with passing places. Drive below the limestone Eglwyseg escarpment and into a wooded area with the cliffs of World's End in front through the trees – be sure to stop and look at the old Elizabethan manor (see below) . Follow the road until it passes through a ford.

Start point: There is a small parking space beyond the ford – grid ref: SJ229479 – or continue to the top of the hill with more parking on your left.

Distance: 1¼ mls (2km) for the basic walk. Several longer possibilities up to 7½ mls (12km).

Map: OS Explorer 255

Grade: Suitable for small children being a short walk at the end of a car ride.

The old Elizabethan black-and-white timbered manor house which you passed on your left on the way to the starting point is on the site of the hunting lodge to which Owain ap Cadwgan carried off the lovely Nest. So, be sure to stop and have a look at it. Today it is called Plas Uchaf and, according to the present owner, Queen Elizabeth I once stayed here, reputedly to have a baby. Winston Churchill and General Goering stayed for a shooting holiday in 1936/37.

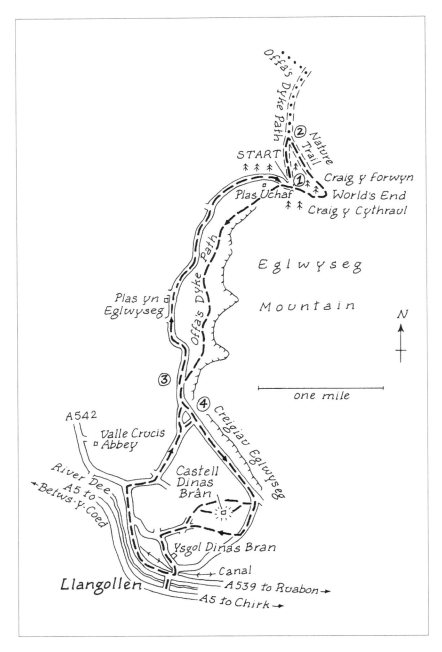

For a pleasant short walk, cross back over the ford and over a stile to an obvious path which goes uphill with the cliffs of Craig y Cythraul – the Devil's Crag – above on your left; the cliffs are called 'World's End' by climbers and the area is now marked on OS maps by the same name. This path is on the line of Offa's Dyke, that extraordinary boundary of bank and ditch built by the king of Mercia four centuries before Owain's love affair with Nest. The path is pleasant and easy to follow – look out for rock climbers on the cliffs. It winds through trees with a couple of small caves just off the path. Eventually you emerge on open hillside. You can return the way you came or, if equipped with a map, can find alternative ways back.

Extension 1: From the highest point (1) on the outward part of the Basic Walk, head north-west through a "Nature Trail" area to join the Offa's Dyke long-distance path (2). Walk north for as long as wished and then return south on the Offa's Dyke route, back to the starting point.

Extension 2: If you have arrived by car and can persuade the driver to take the car back to Llangollen, you can walk south along Offa's Dyke to join the road (3) and *either* walk back along this road to Llangollen (total distance from World's End, 8km) or – even more challenging – shortly after you meet the road, regain the Offa's Dyke route (4) beneath the Eglwyseg escarpment for 1.5km before swinging west to climb up to Castell Dinas Brân (see Walk 3). From here, descend into Llangollen (total distance from World's End, 10km).

2. Corwen: The White Hart of Llangar

Long ago in the peaceful valley of the Afon Dyfrdwy, which Saxons called the River Dee, the pious dwellers in the district of Edeirnion resolved to build a church. It would not be very big (for at that time there were not many people in those parts) but it would be the Church of All Saints, they decided, and built in a place where the Christian folk of the valley could all get to it on Sundays.

Three grey-headed elders took charge of the work and many younger men helped in the carrying of stones and the clearing of the ground. They had chosen a place where the paths from several villages met, a level site that had building materials in plenty ready to hand, and by mustering every man capable of work and starting at dawn of a summer's day they made amazing progress. The first course of huge stones was already in place when darkness fell.

Next morning the builders met again on the site, eager to raise the church walls two or three courses higher. To their utter astonishment, there was no sign of the work they had so well begun the day before. The pile of raw material was still there, but all the stones they had placed in position with so much labour had vanished. It would have needed an army of men to carry the great stones away, so the builders knew that some kind of supernatural agency was at work. After a grave discussion, the three elders gave the word to start building the church again The workers succeeded in regaining all the ground they had lost by this mysterious interference, and went home at nightfall weary but well-content.

On the second morning there was again no sign of their day's work. Every stone had vanished. And again, stubbornly refusing to be frightened or discouraged, they rebuilt the first course of the church walls. On the third morning things were exactly the same – all their work was undone. But this time the three greybeards, after an excited conference, told the church-builders to go to their homes and await word from them. For the elders had discovered that in the night each of them had received the same vision – a bright light shining from above, and a voice saying "Seek the white hart, and where you see him, there build your church". None of the three doubted that only by following this command would they succeed in getting their church finished, and with one accord they set off in different directions to look for the hart, or stag, of this unusual colour.

All that day they wandered, searching, through the woods and thickets that clothed the Berwyn slopes along the valley of the Dyfrdwy river; all that day until darkness was failing, with many a glimpse of the tawny hued deer but never one of a white hart. They had arranged to meet at a place in the river valley near where the Alwen stream flows into the Dyfrdwy, and here at dusk the three came together, tired and despairing. With little spoken, they were about to make their way to their homes when, suddenly, they all saw a great white hart standing on the hillside a little way above the river bank. For an instant he stood, seeming to look down at them; then he vanished, never to reappear.

Next morning, at the summons of the elders, the workmen began to carry the building materials to the place where the hart had stood. When they began to build, the work seemed twice as easy as before and was never interfered with. The walls rose with remarkable speed, the roof seemed almost to grow from the walls, and soon the church was finished.

It was duly sanctified as the Church of All Saints. But to all the people of Edeirnion it was known as Llan-Garw-Gwyn – *garw* meaning 'stag' and *gwyn* meaning 'white'. In later years the name was shortened, becoming first Llangarw and then Llangar. And to this day, the old church, standing in its curious place remote from villages and with no road to it, is called Llangar.

The Walk
Corwen and Llangar Church

How to get there: Corwen is on the A5, approximately 7 miles west of Llangollen. Just to the west of the town (i.e. towards Betws-y-Coed) turn onto the B4401 towards Llandrillo. In about half a mile, the road has grass verges. Look for the rather small sign for the church – the sign is on your left, church on your right – but is difficult to see from your car.

Start point: a section of the old road just before the church sign. Grid ref: SJ063424

Distance: 700 metres in total. Other "real" walks available in the area.

Map: OS Explorer 255

Grade: Short and easy.

The church is normally kept locked and is only open from 13th April to 30th September. Access is by prior arrangement with the custodian at Rug Chapel (01490 412025). This beautiful chapel, just off the A5 west of Corwen, is also well worth a visit.

Cross the road and go down the small lane, opposite the sign, towards the river. You pass a farm on your left where the track turns right then left. Look for a wooden gate here with a sign for the church on the right of the track. Go through the gate and approach the church on a path which enters the churchyard via an ancient lychgate. The church is tiny and although well kept is now disused. You can obtain the key as described or get a good look at the interior from a large window in the far (east) end. The churchyard is a chaos of aged tombstones and the tall yew tree must be very old, but it is a peaceful and lovely spot with the River Dee winding just below.

Bonus walk: Corwen is a good centre for walks. A short but

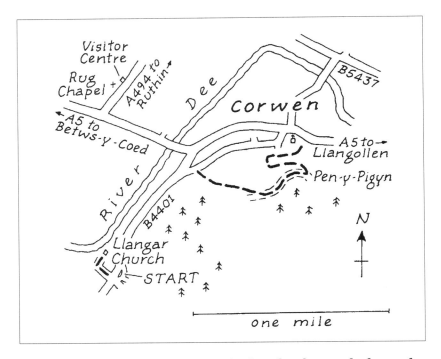

steep one is along the footpath that leads south from the church in the town (i.e. not Llangar church). This zig-zags up to Pen y Pigyn, also known as Glyndower's Seat, some 800ft above the town and gives excellent views over the Dee valley.

3. Llangollen: Myfanwy of Dinas Brân

The old story-spinners told of a hero named Brân who built a dinas, or city, on the great mound above the Dyfrdwy vale; and that was as long ago as the Bronze Age. The centuries rolled by, and there came one of the Lords of Ial (a forerunner of the Yale who founded the great American college) to make a more habitable fortress on the ditches and parapets of the old dinas. By about the year 1250 a stone castle began to rise on the great mound, every stone of its walls carried to the summit by gangs of serfs or prisoners. Castell Dinas Brân was the work of the Norman barons who were determined to subdue the rebellious Welsh.

But there were treaties and agreements – even intermarrying – between the great Welsh families and the Norman nobles. And 100 years after the building of Castell Dinas Brân the fortress was held by a Vychan of the house of Tudor Trevor, whose overlord was the Norman Earl of Arundel and whose daughter Myfanwy was the most beautiful maiden in all the land of Powys.

Myfanwy was well aware of her beauty, but like many a pretty girl before and since, she liked nothing better than to hear her beauty praised. Many men, young and handsome, warriors and of good birth, thronged the hall of Castell Dinas Brân to seek her favour. Myfanwy Vychan spurned them all, for they lacked the things she most desired – the gifts of weaving, poetry and music that reflected as in a mirror her wondrous beauty. The one man who possessed these gifts was a youthful bard, penniless and of lowly birth, who dwelt in the valley below the castle. His name was Hywel ap Einion.

Hywel had fallen madly in love with Myfanwy, and every

day he toiled up the long, steep ascent to the castle with his harp, hoping to be admitted to the hall where he could play and sing to Myfanwy Vychan. Sometimes he would be allowed to enter, sometimes he was sent away. But whenever he was admitted to Myfanwy's presence he played and sang to her so wonderfully – always praising her unrivalled beauty in a flood of wild words and enchanting music – in the hope that she would neither listen to, nor look at, any man other than Hywel ap Einion. And the young bard came to believe that she returned his love.

Too soon his hope was shattered. A suitor more hand-some, more powerful, and (perhaps) more articulate than the others came wooing. The match was a suitable one for the heiress of the Trevors and, in the ensuing betrothal, festivi-ties the poor bard was quite forgotten. There was not a word for him nor even a look, from the beauty of Castell Dinas Brân by way of farewell.

Hywel climbed no more to the castle on the hilltop. Broken-hearted, he wandered through the Dyfrdwy forests with his harp; and as he went, he composed the ode which was to live for more than 400 years as one of the best-loved Welsh poems. It was a very long ode, and of its many lines four can be translated into English thus:

> *'Far from Myfanwy's marble towers*
> *I pass my solitary hours.*
> *O thou that shinest like the sky,*
> *Behold thy faithful Hywel die!'*

But Hywel did not die of his broken heart. And, as for the cruel Myfanwy's Vychan, to whom he sang –

> *'Fairer thou and colder too,*
> *Than winter snow on Aran's brow'* –

Her undeserved reward was to be made famous by her humble lover's poem. So to this day, when Castell Dinas Brân is a lifeless ruin, her story lives on.

The Walk
Llangollen and Castell Dinas Brân

How to get there: Llangollen is on the A5, between Corwen and Chirk. It can also be approached from the north on the A542. If coming from the Betws-y-Coed direction, enter the town on the A5 and turn off left at the traffic lights, the car park is up a side street on your left.

Start point: Public car park in cenre of town.
Grid ref: SJ223431.

Distance: 2 mls or 2½ mls (3km or 4km) depending on whether you walk there and back or use the alternative return path.

Map: OS Explorer 255

Grade: Steep paths, fine views. Allow about 90 minutes there and back.

From the car park, turn right, then left to cross the bridge over the River Dee. Once over the bridge, turn right then immediately left up Wharf Hill. Go up the hill and across the bridge over the canal. Opposite this bridge is a footpath with a sign to Castell Dinas Brân. The path climbs past the school, called Ysgol Dinas Brân, and goes through a kissing gate then across a small lane and continues directly opposite. Go up the path and through another kissing gate, then up another lane, which soon comes to a crossroads. Cross straight over these to the unsurfaced lane opposite. After 50 yards, pass through yet another kissing gate to emerge on to open hillside with the old castle above you. Follow the obvious zigzag path, which climbs steeply to the summit in about 25 minutes.

Once you reach the ruins, take care with small children, as in some places there are nasty small drops that fall onto very steep hillsides. There is not much left of the castle and it is anyone's guess where the castle hall used to be that saw

Hywel ap Einion's musical courtship of Myfanwy Vychan. But the views are magnificent and from here, 1060ft above sea level, can be seen Llangollen and the Dee valley, the Berwyn mountains and the Shropshire plains plus the man-made landmarks of Telford's aqueduct and William-son's aqueduct.

Extension: For an alternative way back, exit on the far side of the castle and follow the signs down the hillside until you join with a small lane, turn right (2) to end back at the canal bridge.

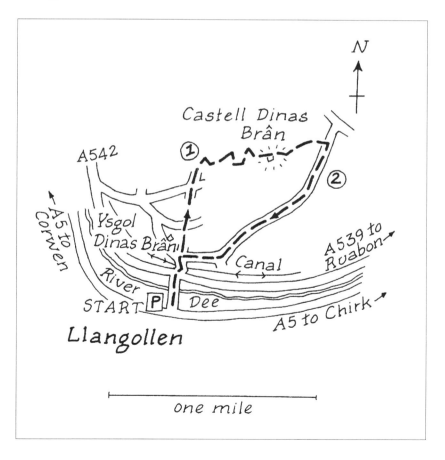

The Conwy Valley

4. Betws-y-Coed: The Legend of the Afanc

Long ago, before histories began to be written, the people of the Vale of Conwy were sorely troubled by a monster that lived in a pool of the river. This *afanc*, as he was called, was an enormous beast that possessed supernatural powers, which he used (when he was in a vicious mood) to cause disastrous floods, ruining the crops and drowning the cattle. Spear, dart and sword had been tried against him by the bravest of the young men, but no weapon forged by man could make any impression on the afanc's scaly hide. The greybeards held conference, and decided that there was only one thing to do: the monster must be removed from his pool and taken far away to some other lake beyond the mountains.

Preparations began at once. Strong iron chains were forged, and the two mightiest oxen in the land – the giant long-horned animals belonging to Hu Gadarn – were brought to Betws-y-Coed, for the afanc pool was close to this place. But the problem of how to get the afanc out of the pool, so that he could be chained to the oxen, had still to be solved. Now the monster was known to be very partial to beautiful maidens, showing in this at least one human quality; and when this was remembered, a courageous damsel was found who agreed to act as decoy. The lake to which the afanc was to be dragged was chosen – Llyn Ffynnon Las, under the peak of Snowdon – and all was ready. The giant oxen and the men with the chains hid themselves in the woods near the pool while the damsel sat by the water's edge and called softly to the afanc. By-and-by the hideous monster came wallowing up out of the depths, and – yielding to the girl's enticements – heaved himself ashore and laid his ugly head in her lap. Now, or never, was the moment! The men leaped from their

concealment and deftly wound the chains round the afanc, who saw too late the trick that had been played upon him. Furious, he struck at the girl with his great claws, tearing her breast, and hurled himself back into the pool.

But the chains were already harnessed to the oxen, and slowly, with every man present lending his strength to help, the afanc was drawn out. All up the rocky Lledr valley they dragged him, as far as the spot where Dolwyddelan stands now; and striking north-west over the shoulder of Moel Siabod they crossed the watershed and came into the head of the Gwynant valley. So great were the efforts of the oxen that the eye of one of them dropped out, causing it to shed floods of tears which formed the pool called ever afterwards Pwll Llygad yr Ych, the Pool of the Ox's Eye.

The last part of the oxen's labour was the hardest. They dragged the afanc up into Gwm Dyli, past Llyn Llydaw, and at last reached the lake, 1,970 ft above sea-level, which is now called Glaslyn but whose proper name is Llyn Ffynnon Las, the Lake of the Blue Fountain. On the shores of the lake, with Snowdon summit frowning overhead, the men loosed the chains. The monster plunged headlong into Glaslyn at once, and sank from sight in the immensely deep blue water. And there, the old folk of the area will tell you, he dwells to this day.

The Walk

Betws-y-Coed to Afanc Pool

How to get there: Betws-y-Coed is on the A5, near to where it meets the A470.

Start point: the car park by the station at Betws-y-Coed. Grid ref: SH795566

Distance: basic route, 2½ mls (4km). Can be extended to Fairy Glen. Longer circular route of 4½ mls (7km).

Map: OS Outdoor Leisure 17

Grade: Short and easy. Circular route is moderate.

From the car park, head back towards the A5 and turn left for about 200 yards. Just before the road crosses the railway, a minor road turns uphill to your right (1) and in a short while you pass the village garage, Betws Motors. Follow this road, which quickly leaves the houses behind and becomes a leafy lane. You pass under a railway bridge (2) that carries the single-track line to Blaenau Ffestiniog, one of the most beautiful railway trips in Britain, and soon the lane is running along the bank of the River Conwy. There is more than one fine pool but the Afanc Pool (sometimes called Beaver Pool) is the big one near the junction of the lane with the A470, which crosses the river by a stone bridge (3).

The Afanc Pool is large and deep and rather gloomy under its big trees. No description of an Afanc has been left by the people who have claimed to have seen one, but no doubt he was a horrific monster and on any but the brightest of days the pool looks a suitable home for him. A small path leads down to its shore and, as there is no Afanc, there now it is safe to go down.

Extension 1: This walk is worth extending to Fairy Glen, as the entrance to this famous beauty spot is only a couple of minutes from Afanc Pool. Go to the junction with the A470 and turn left over the bridge, then cross over and follow the sign-posted lane immediately beyond the bridge next to the Fairy Glen Hotel. The lane brings you to Fairy Glen in about 15 minutes easy walking. When you arrive, take great care with small children on the descent into Fairy Glen, especially if the river is high – there have been accidents here. Note that a small admission fee is charged.

Extension 2: For those who like further exploration there is another little route. Having crossed the bridge and taken the Fairy Glen lane, look for a small gap in the right-hand wall. If you go through the gap a small path takes you down to the riverbank, turn left and you will come to some water-worn rock scenery by a big pool where the River Lledr joins the Conwy. If you turn right you can scramble under the arch of the road bridge to a fine rock seat overlooking the Afanc Pool. When the river is high you can see white water canoeists here on a trip down the Conwy.

Extension 3: If you are an experienced walker **and** if you have the Ordnance Survey map for the area, here is a suggested return route. From where the lane passes under the railway (2) a path initially runs to the right (i.e. west) of the line to head steeply over the mountain to Llyn Elsi. At the top of the hill, continue due west and you hit the dam at the southern end of Llyn Elsi (4). Another path from the top of the hill leads to a point half-way along the lake – it does not really matter which one you take. In either case, turn right and walk alongside the lake. Then, leave the water's edge near the northern end of the lake (5) to head north for 500m before bearing right (east) to join the Jubilee Path. This leads through the forest and down to the A5, approx 200m west (6) of the Pont y Pair bridge.

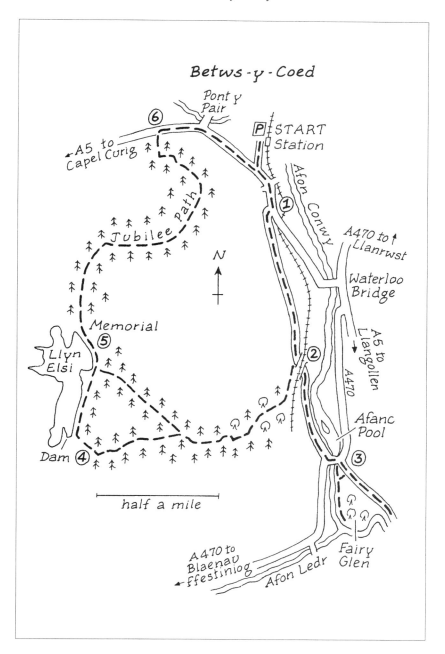

5. Penmaenmawr:
The Stone Women of Moelfre

In the fields by the shores of Conwy Bay, the corn had been harvested. The oxen had trodden the grain from the ears, and the chaff and the grain lay together waiting to be winnowed. The winnowing was done by the women, who would have to work for hour after hour, tossing up the chaff and grain into the wind so that the lighter chaff would be blown away and the heavier grain left ready for the miller. But for days there had not been a breath of wind in the fields by the sea. Only on the tall hills that curved round to the headland of Penmaenmawr was there any wind.

The women grew impatient. The rain might come, soaking grain and chaff together, and rob them of the good flour from which they made their bread.

"There's plenty of wind up on Moelfre," said one woman, who wore a red kirtle (a traditional short working skirt). "Let's carry the corn in sacks and winnow it up there."

She said this on a Sunday, and in Wales no man, woman, or child was ever to be seen working on this day of rest.

"We would be breaking the Sabbath," said another, whose kirtle was white.

"What then?" retorted her neighbour. "Doesn't the wind blow on a Sunday, and shall we waste it and lose the good flour?"

"That's sense," nodded a third woman, in a blue kirtle. "I'll get three sacks and we three will carry the corn up to Moelfre."

So the three women filled the sacks and started up the hillside, bent beneath their loads. They passed a cottage, and here an old man called loudly after them, warning them that they sinned in breaking the Sabbath and would be punished.

Higher up they passed a farm, and here the farmer came out to give them the same solemn warning. The three laden women laughed at the warnings and toiled on.

They climbed the steep glen where once men had used the hard Graig Lwyd stone to make primitive axes. They gained the lofty crest where the Meini Hirion – the Long Stones —stood in a wide circle. There was still no wind, but the round summit called Moelfre was not far away and they knew there would be wind up there. They carried their sacks to the very top of the hill, emptied them in a heap, and began the winnowing, throwing up the corn into the steady breeze that was blowing there.

And then came the dreadful happening which Sir John Wynn recorded in his book published in the 17th century: "These faythles women, regardynge there profytt more than the obsearvynge of God's commandments," were instantly turned into three stones, one red, one white, and one blue.

There are no coloured stones on the top of Moelfre now. But a little searching will reveal, sunk in the turf of the summit, the tops of three grey rocks; as if the Stone Women of Moelfre had at last been permitted to sink into the very ground.

The Walk

Penmaenmawr to Moelfre and the Druids' Circle

How to get there: The start is in Penmaenmawr, 3½ miles west of Conwy.

Start point: main car park on the seaward side of the A55 Expressway. Grid ref: SH718768.

Distance: 5 mls (8km)

Map: OS Outdoor Leisure 17

Grade: This walk ascends to 1,423ft so is not really suitable for small children.

From the main car park, walk through the underpass and along Paradise Road. Cross Ffordd Bangor and, after just a few metres, turn right into Y Berllan. Follow the road around to the left to where two tracks lead inland and take the left-hand track. This path mounts gently into a green valley under steep hillsides; high on your right are the quarries of Graig Lwyd. You soon reach a minor road, called Craig Lwyd, turn right (1) until you come to a farmhouse on your left with a footpath sign going to the left of the house. Look for a small way-marked gate on your right above the farm, go through it and continue up the path. Down on the left are the moulds and scars where primitive man extracted the stone for the 'Graig Lwyd' axes; stone axes that undoubtedly came from Penmaenmawr have been found all over Britain.

At the head of the valley, the path goes left over a stream and across a narrow concrete causeway. Walk to the wall ahead (2), where a signpost stands. Go through this and turn right to walk uphill with the wall on your right. Join a broader footpath, the North Wales Way, and turn right along it. In a few minutes, you reach a level space on the crest of the hills with the domed hill of Moelfre just above and an easy

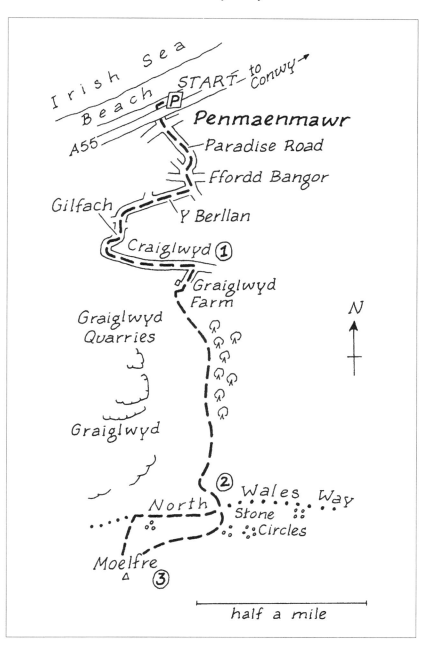

200ft climb brings you to its summit (3). The height here is 1,423ft with fine views.

The non-appearance of the Stone Women may be disappointing but Meini Hirion (Grid reference SH722746) will make up for it. This Druids' Circle of stones is one of the finest in Wales and is only ten minutes from Moelfre. Descend the hill and follow the path that runs nearly level along the crest, with the sea on your left. Soon you will come to a circle of rocks close on the right of the path; these are also primitive remains but those of Meini Hirion are a short distance further. The circle of rocks may be as much as 4,000 years old and was probably an early form of observatory. However, it was undoubtedly used as a place of sacrifice in the early Bronze Age, for investigators discovered in an urn at the centre of the circle the cremated remains of a child with a bronze knife.

You can extend this walk with the aid of a map but without this, it is best to return the same way.

6. Llyn Geirionydd: Taliesin the Bard

Elphin, son of Gwyddno Garanhir, was the unluckiest prince in all the history of Wales. His father, who ruled over Mid Wales in the 6th century, gave him a large province as his estate but almost immediately the sea broke the defensive dams of that estate and it was lost beneath the waves. By way of comforting him, Gwyddno presented his unfortunate young man with the annual salmon-netting of the Dovey river, which was the equivalent of giving him a large present of money, so vast was the number of salmon usually caught. But Elphin's bad luck stayed with him. As he watched the river-keeper and his servants working the nets, he saw that there was not a single fish in them. Indeed, the only object to emerge from the river was a large leather bag that had lodged on the edge of the weir. It was a thousand chances to one that there was anything of worth in the leather bag, but Elphin bade the river-keeper bring it to him. This was done and the bag was opened. Inside was a small boy, hardly more than a babe, but very much alive.

"Tal-iesin!" exclaimed the river-keeper; which means 'How radiant is his brow!': for the child's forehead seemed to shine with a strange lustre.

"Taliesin let him be called," said Elphin, and set the boy on his horse, and rode homeward with him, sadly at first but soon in wonder and amazement.

As they rode, the child began to speak, holding forth in an impassioned ode. This miraculous poetry told Elphin that the boy had been sent to guide him; that he was to be not only a great poet but also a great prophet and, before him, all Elphin's enemies should fall.

The years passed, and from that time Elphin prospered in all he did. As for Taliesin, he became the most famous bard of

Britain. Among the prophecies was that which foretold the end of the wicked king Maelgwn Gwynedd, but his most inspired odes were those that urged on the warriors of Britain in their struggle against the Saxon invaders.

Many places in Wales became associated with the name Taliesin, especially the beautiful lake called Geirionydd, on the forested heights above the Conwy valley. Here in his later years the bard used to come to meditate and seek inspiration.

To this day the sayings of this first and greatest of bards are remembered in Wales, and none more so than the famous prophecy he made, towards the end of his life, about the British of that time and their fate:

> *'Their Lord they shall praise,*
> *Their language they shall keep,*
> *Their land they shall lose – except wild Wales.'*

The Walk

Llyn Geirionydd (between Betws-y-Coed and LLanrwst)

How to get there: From Betws-y-Coed, go over the old Pont y Pair bridge on the B5106. Continue to Gwydir Castle and take a left turn up a small road sign-posted to Llyn Geirionydd; if you hit the 'T' junction a few metres further on you have gone too far. Follow this road and take the first turning to the right signposted to Llanrhychwyn, this is the start of the walk so park your car here. You may have to continue a few metres up the Geirionydd road and park in the spaces on left-hand side. An alternative parking place is on the B5106 – see map.

The start point is also very near to the large village of **Llanrwst** which has ample pubs, tea shops and other facilities. You could leave your car here if you don't mind the extra 2km of walking. In any event, it is well worth calling here for a stroll by the river either before or after the main walk.

Start point: See above. Grid reference for first parking place: SH789609.

Distance: 6¼ mls (10km)

Map: OS Outdoor Leisure 17

Grade: This moderate walk takes about four hours. A pleasant day out with picnic.

This is longer than most legend walks. Except for a suggested short cut, it is possible to do the whole thing by car but it is well worth the walking effort.

From the recommended start point, the lane is easy walking and climbs steeply up into the forest. Twenty minutes of this and the angle eases as you emerge into an upper land of fields and streams. Here is a tiny hamlet called Tai (1), not named but shown on the OS maps, where a signpost directs you to Llyn Geirionydd. In ten minutes a right turn, also

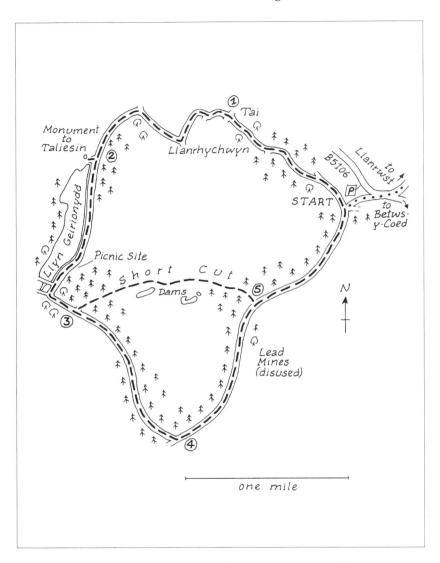

sign-posted, brings you past a farm and downhill to the lake. There are some gates on this section – please close them behind you. This stretch is delightful: mountains in the distance and the Crafnant Valley far down to the right with Llyn Geirionydd coming into view slowly on the left.

The lake beneath its fine crags and forests looks more Tyroleon or Bavarian than Welsh. As you approach the end of the lake, there is the stone monument to Taliesin (2), erected on the place where the bard lived for a long time. The monument is reached, through a kissing gate, some five minutes from the road. There is a small inscription on it, placed there when it was rebuilt in the mid-seventies.

Return to the road and follow the lake shore with lots of picnic places and, at the far end, a forestry picnic site with tables and chairs. At the far end of the lake turn left, opposite a farmhouse; the lane climbs uphill past some old lead mines with fine backward views. At the top of the ascent, there is a glimpse of Moel Siabod on the right and then there is a fifteen-minute walk between trees. Continue until a 'T' junction is reached (4). Turn left here for the last bit of uphill past more lead mines – it is worth stopping to have a quick look around. The forest here is full of lead mines – some are massive and very dangerous, but this small area has information signs and is safe.

Continue along road to the highest point of your walk, downhill down past a small lake, sometimes dry in summer, with more lead mines including a chimney on your right. Then walk steeply downhill for about a mile to your parking place.

For a short cut (cutting almost 2km off the circuit, as you walk along the lane from the monument, after 200m there is a forest track to the left (3). Head along this almost due west for almost 2km until you hit the lane (5) where you turn left for the last 1.5km back to your start point.

The North Coast

7.
Rhôs-on-Sea: The End of Maelgwn Gwynedd

8.
Rhôs-on-Sea: How Prince Madoc Discovered America

9.
Deganwy and its Castle

7. Rhôs-on-Sea: The End of Maelgwn Gwynedd

Of all the princes who have ruled over Gwynedd, as North Wales was once called, the most wicked was Maelgwn. He was Prince of Gwynedd thirteen centuries ago, and this is his story.

In those days there were four petty kingdoms in Wales, and the four rulers wished to decide which of them should be Brenhin Pennaf, or chief king. It was agreed that they should meet on the sands of the Dovey estuary, bringing their thrones with them; that the thrones should be placed in a row fronting the incoming tide, with their royal owners sitting on them; and that whichever of the four stayed longest on his throne when the sea came racing in to submerge them should be declared Brenhin Pennaf.

Now Maelgwn had a cunning counsellor, Maeldav the Elder, who was determined that his master should triumph. "Maeldav," says the old chronicle, "secretly prepared a throne made of wings" – though we can take it as pretty certain that these were inflated skins, to act as water-wings. At any rate, the spring tide came roaring and foaming in, and the sea rose higher and higher, until the princes from Powys and South Wales took fright and splashed their way to safety. But Maelgwn rode the waves on his floating throne, and so became chief ruler of Wales.

It was an age when men were accustomed to harsh treatment from their overlords, but Maelgwn Gwynedd overstepped all bounds of cruelty. The people of his own land cursed him for the blackness of his deeds, but there was no one strong enough to oppose him and it seemed as if the sufferings of his many victims would never be avenged. He built himself a palace close to the north coast, within

bowshot of a hill-fort that had been the stronghold of his ancestors hundreds of years earlier, and here at Llys Rhos (as it was called), Maelgwn lived a life of drunkenness and excess, with other evil-doing too horrible to be told.

At last the great bard and prophet Taliesin foretold an end to the suffering of Gwynedd. This was his prophecy: "A wondrous beast shall come up from Moda Rhianedd, the Sea march of the Maidens, to avenge the iniquities of Maelgwn. Its hair and its teeth and its eyes shall all be yellow, and this beast shall be the end of Maelgwn Gwynedd!"

The prophecy of Taliesin was fulfilled in the year 547. In that year the deadly plague, which some called the Yellow Death, was ravaging Europe, and spread northward into Britain. As the plague's trail of death approached the land of Gwynedd, Maelgwn's terror of it grew until he was almost mad with fear. He shut himself in his palace of Llys Rhos with a few favourite courtiers and forbade anyone to pass in or out, and for a little while it seemed that he had escaped the fate that was overtaking so many of his subjects in the world outside. But one day, hearing his name loudly called from the outer gateway, Maelgwn looked through the keyhole of the great door. A moment later he fell to the ground, writhing in agony; and his only words before he died were "The Yellow Beast!"

The terrified courtiers fled, leaving their dead prince in the palace. And it was long indeed before anyone would venture in to bring out the body of the Brenhin Pennaf for burial; which gave rise to a saying that is remembered to this day: Hir hun y Faelgwn yn Llys Rhos – 'the long sleep of Maelgwn in the palace of Rhos'.

Llys Rhos fell into ruin. But from its stones a new palace named Llys Euryn was built, on the very spot where Maelgwn Gwynedd wrought – and paid for – his evil deeds.

The Walk

Rhôs-on-Sea to Llys Euryn and Bryn Euryn

How to get there: Rhôs-on-Sea is just north of the A55, a mile or so east of Colwyn Bay.

Start point: Grid ref: SH803835.

Distance: a few hundred metres, but steep ones!

Map: OS Outdoor Leisure 17

Grade: All right for children. About 1 hour with a steep last section.

From the centre of Rhôs sea-front, look out for Rhos Road, then follow it uphill past the shops and soon you come to some traffic lights. Cross over the main road and continue straight on to another crossroads. Once again cross over and follow the small lane opposite. 50 yards up this, park in a small car park next to a quarry; there is an information board in the car park. Walk back down the lane for a few yards to a stepped path on your left with a notice to Bryn Euryn, and follow the path which soon leads to the old ruin of Llys Euryn. The building that can be seen today was constructed in the 15th century for the eldest son of Gruffyd Goch, leader of one of the old tribal divisions of Wales. It was a very large house for the times and was built to be defended. At this time, the Wars of the Roses were in progress and Wales was a place of conflict. This was probably the site of the 13th century hall of Ednyfed Fyclan, which was of timber construction.

From Llys Euryn, exit to your left and follow a path above the quarry, you will soon emerge into an open area with views back towards Little Orme. Look for a marker post with a figure 4 on it, turn sharp left here with the path going uphill through a small wood. At a junction, again follow the path to the left. Continue uphill heading for the highest point and emerge on a bald hillside with some shrubs on the top. Climb steeply over grass to these shrubs, which are best taken on the right. Just above the shrubs, hidden from below, is an Ordnance Survey cairn. Although only a little over 400ft there is a splendid panorama, which makes it seem much higher, with views of the coast and the mountains of Snowdonia – a great place for a picnic on a sunny day. Flower enthusiasts will see, in summer, much limestone flora including rock rose, scabious, harebell and traveller's joy. You will need some imagination to trace the blurred outline of the hill fortress that occupied this site but it must have been an impregnable defensive position before the days of gunpowder. To descend, retrace your steps until you arrive at a large white house on your right, here you can turn right and follow the lane directly back to your car.

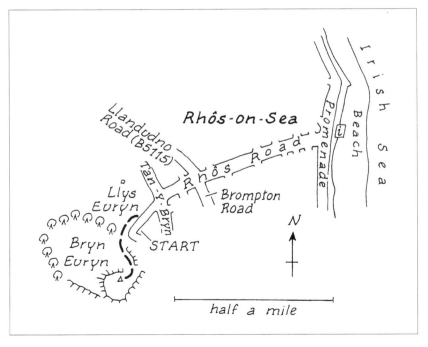

8. Rhôs-on-Sea: How Prince Madoc discovered America

Owain Gwynedd, ruler of North Wales in the 12th century, had nineteen sons. One of them was Idwal, whose story is told later in this book. Another was Madoc, who loved the sea better than the mountains of his own land. But the two princes of greatest importance were Howel and Dafydd, for Owain their father had resolved that between them they should rule Gwynedd after his death.

Owain died in December 1169; and the recorded date reminds us that he and his sons were historical persons. On his death, Howel and Dafydd, like many other kings' sons in history, quarrelled as to which should be the more powerful force in the kingdom and thus began a civil war, turning Gwynedd from a peaceful country into a land of strife. Now Prince Madoc was a peace-loving man, a thinker and a poet rather than a warrior. His courage and hardihood had been shown by several daring voyages, but he had no mind to win fame in battles, least of all by joining with Dafydd or Howel to fight against a brother. Each of the warring princes wished him +to declare himself on their side, for Madoc was well loved by all who lived on the coasts of Gwynedd. To escape from this unhappy situation, Madoc determined to carry out an adventure he had long considered. This was to sail westward beyond Ireland (where his brother Riryd had an estate) until he came to another land beyond the ocean, or – which was just as likely – until his ship met her fate in the unknown waters of the edge of the world.

So Prince Madoc at once rigged and manned the famous *Gwennan Gorn*, a ship of which little detail is known except that her planks were joined with stag's horns instead of nails and that Madoc had voyaged in her to distant islands in the northern sea. She was built of oak from the forests of Nant Gwynant, says one bard; and another, Gynfric ap Gronow, wrote:

> *Gwennan Gorn, brought to the Gele*
> *To be given a new mast,*
> *Was taken then to the quay of Afon Ganol*
> *For Madoc's famous voyage.*

For in those days the north coast of Gwynedd (where Colwyn Bay and Abergele stand today) had two small seaports at the river-mouths of the Gele and the Ganol. And from the quay of the Afon Ganol, in the year 1170, the *Gwennan Gorn* sailed on her great adventure.

It is recorded that Madoc's brother Riryd joined the ship at Lundy Island. She departed westward, and for several years nothing was heard of her. Then – and no one can be sure how long afterwards – the *Gwennan Gorn* came back. She had barely enough men on board to sail her, for all the rest had been left in the new land that Madoc had discovered after many weeks' sail across the western ocean. The Prince stayed in Gwynedd only long enough to gather a fleet of ten small ships and fill them with volunteers, both men and women, who would sail with him to the new land and make a new Gwynedd there.

The ten ships sailed, having collected at Lundy Island. And this time they were never heard of again, unless the evidence of 600 years later is to be believed. For during the 17th and 18th centuries, when the wilderness of North America was being opened up by the pioneers, reports began to come in of a large tribe of 'Red' Indians – the Mandans – whose skins were white and who spoke a language very similar to Welsh. This began a long period of exhaustive research which brought other old records to light; and on the testimony of these a great many people believe that Prince Madoc landed in Alabama in 1170, thus discovering North America

more than 300 years before Columbus. In 1953 a large memo-
rial tablet was erected on the shore of Mobile Bay, Alabama,
bearing these words:

*'In memory of Prince Madoc, a Welsh explorer, who landed
on the shores of Mobile Bay in 1170 and left behind, with the
Indians, the Welsh language.'*

The Walk

Rhôs-on-Sea, Llandrillo and Penrhyn Bay

How to get there: Starting from Llandudno, exit the town on the coast road heading for Colwyn Bay. After skirting the Little Orme, stick on the coast to Rhôs-on-Sea. Drive along the promenade, looking for the golf course on your right; soon after this, look out for Trillo Avenue also on your right, and park on the roadside just beyond Trillo Avenue.

Start point: see above – Grid ref: SH812842.

Distance: 1¼ mls (2km)

Map: no map needed

Grade: Easy walking on pavements.

For this simple trip, no sketch map is provided: you simply need to know where to look rather than where to go as nothing is the same as when Madoc sailed. From the suggested parking place in Trillo Avenue, walk back towards Llandudno on the seaward side of the road. Look out for a small chapel on your right; this is the smallest in Wales and bears the notice:

'Parish of Llandrillo yn Rhos. All reverence is due to this sacred spot. This chapel is built over the holy well of St Trillo a Celtic saint of the 6th century. Pilgrim turn in and offer prayer the Lord be with you.'

Even if you are not a pilgrim it is worth a look, though unfortunately in these times it has to be kept locked. For the memento of Madoc, walk on for another ten minutes with good views of the Little Orme head jutting out into Penrhyn Bay. The golf course soon appears on your left. Cross the road and the last house before the golf course is a big one called Odstone. Looking into the garden, you will see two pools – these are what was once the river bed of the Afon Ganol where Madoc's ship lay alongside the quay. On the left, as you look in the garden, is an old stone wall – this is all that remains of the quay. There is an inscribed tablet on it, now hard to spot in the shrubs, which reads:

'Prince Madoc sailed from here Aber Kerrick Gwynan,
1170 AD and landed at Mobile, Alabama with his ships
Gorn Gwynant and Pedr Sant.'

It will be noticed that this version speaks of two ships and has a different spelling for Gwennan Gorn. Now you have seen the actual place from where he sailed, don't you feel that Prince Madoc may have beaten Columbus to it after all?

Please note that this garden is private so on no account should it be entered without the owner's consent.

9. Deganwy and its Castle

Sometime in the early centuries AD, two holy women of
Ireland, Modwenna and Bride, were sitting in a meadow
close to the Irish shore with their servants Luge and Athea.
Suddenly, all four found themselves at sea – for the portion
of the Emerald Isle they were on had broken away from the
mainland. They floated eastward for a day and a night before
their drifting island grounded on the shores of Britain at the
mouth of a river. The river was the Conwy, and the piece of
Ireland (which quickly became part of the coast) was the
peninsula of Deganwy.

Modwenna settled in Mercia where, as Saint Modwenna
of the Forest of Arden, she wrote the story of this miraculous

journey. Saint Bride – or Sant Ffraidd, which is the Welsh form of her name – stayed in western Britain, and is commemorated by the village two miles farther up the estuary, Llansantffraidd Glan Conwy.

Many hundreds of years later, the Norman conquerors of Britain built a castle on the rocky hill above Deganwy. For a long time Deganwy Castle was the limit of the Norman advance against the rebel Welsh princes, the object of fierce attacks and desperate defences. One of the first Norman lords to occupy it was Robert, Earl of Rhuddlan, who was sent there with a small force of men-at-arms to establish the Norman idea of law and order. One morning – it was July 3rd, 1088 – news reached the castle of a marauding force raiding from the mountains higher up the Conwy. The Earl sent his tiny army to deal with it, under command of his lieutenant, while he himself remained in the castle with one knight and a few servants.

At noon of that day, Robert of Rhuddlan 'was taking his midday sleep in the Castle, with no thought of danger or of warlike alarms', when a frightened messenger toiled up to the castle gate to beg the Earl for help. Three ships, Welsh raiders from farther along the coast, were beached on the sands below Great Ormes Head. The men from them had seized women and cattle and were only waiting for the tide to carry them off with their plunder. Earl Robert leaped from his bed and ordered all his retainers to follow him to the shore without a moment's delay. But when he rode out of the gateway, wearing no armour but with sword in hand, only his one knight followed him. They galloped down the steep path to the shore, came up to the three ships just as the tide was beginning to lift them, and demanded that the cattle and prisoners should be put ashore. The pirates replied with a shower of arrows and javelins. And Robert of Rhuddlan and his brave companion fell from their horses, dead.

For nearly two centuries after this event Deganwy Castle,

was attacked and defended, destroyed and rebuilt. Not until the year 1284, when King Edward I completed the building of Conwy Castle on the opposite shore of the estuary, did the invading armies from England make much progress against the stubborn bravery of the Welsh. And by that time the little fortress on the rocky hill had fallen into disuse and was soon to become a ruin.

The Walk
Deganwy Castle

How to get there: Deganwy is 2 miles from the centre of Llandudno. Follow the A546 from Llandudno and, when you enter Deganwy, look for the Deganwy Castle Hotel on your right.

Start point: small car park about 50m past the hotel on your right. Grid ref: SH778792.

Distance: The basic walk is 1 mile (1.5km), there and back, but can be extended to a 1½ mile (2.5km) circular route.

Map: OS Outdoor Leisure 17

Grade: Easy. The basic walk takes just one hour. Care needed near the top with small children.

Exit the car park on foot and turn left, then take a right turn called York Road. Follow the road (which becomes Gannock Park) for five minutes and look for a public footpath on your left. Take this path between two walls and exit, via a gate, onto open hillside. From here, go straight on keeping the small crags on your left with a wire fence to your right; you can catch glimpses of parts of the old castle at the top of the crags. If you expect a castle like those at Conwy or Harlech you will be sadly disappointed. What you are visiting is an older fortress and what you are seeing is the ghost of a castle that was built here a thousand years ago.

Follow the fence until a path bears up to your left to a grassy dip or 'saddle' between two rock horns. When you reach the saddle, there is a part of one of the old castle walls and a stone plaque showing the position of the gatehouse. You can see now this was a natural fortification, the crags on each side were here long before man, and all the Normans had to do was build the walls in between. Beyond the stone plaque follow a small path up to your left which contours the crag. This follows the hillside, climbing steadily, with the wire fence you followed now 100ft below to your left. **Be careful here with small children – do not let them run ahead as there are sheer cliffs in front of you.**

Continue on the path to the summit. There are no battlements left now, just small sections of walls. But what a wonderful defensive position this must have been, much better than the later Conwy castle. The views all around are magnificent for such a short climb, with Conwy castle and marina looking like child's toys and, in the distance, the Carneddau mountains with the second highest peak in Wales, Carnedd Llewelyn. Looking the other way, north, Llandudno is spread like a town plan with Great Ormes Head protecting it like another bigger fortress.

For the descent, go down the same way until you reach the grassy saddle, turn left here and down grass slopes to a path running round the slopes. Turn left again under the crags, and soon the orecipitous wall of Castle Crag appears above to your left showing the largest area of man-made wall still remaining, with part of a turret on its right. The path quickly leads back to the gate and public footpath where you regain Gannock Park.

Extension: the walk can be lengthened by approximately 1km as follows: continue past the castle and along the footpath that leads to Maes-y-Castell (1). From this point, head back south along a footpath with the castle mound visible to your right. After 0.5km, at a junction of paths (2), bear right to a viewpoint. Follow the path from here to where you initially began the ascent on the outward section of the walk.

Bangor and Menai

10. Anglesey:
The Isle of St Seiriol

No two Saints were ever more friendly than St Cybi and St Seiriol. Both of these holy men lived on the Isle of Anglesey (Ongul's Ey as it was then called) in the 6th century; but Cybi lived in the north-west, where Holyhead now stands, and Seiriol lived in the extreme eastern corner nearly 30 miles away. It is told of them that, for many years, they met every day at the Wells of Clorach, halfway between Caer Gybi – where Cybi was building a church – and Penmon where Seiriol had his cell. Cybi walked 15 miles south-eastward, with the sun of morning and noon on his face, and Seiriol walked 15 miles north-westward with the sun behind him. When they parted to walk home again, the sun had crossed the sky. As a consequence, Cybi became dark and sunburned while Seiriol remained pale and fair. To this day they are called, Cybi Felyn (Cybi of the Tawny Hue) and Seiriol Wyn (Seiriol the Fair).

In their later years these meetings ceased, for Cybi was increasingly devoted to his church in the north. So famous had the man and his work become that the northern headland was called Holy Head by the outlanders, though to the Welsh it was still known as Caergybi.

Seiriol, meanwhile, was equally renowned for his holiness and his inspired teaching. It is said that the Norse settlers who then inhabited much of Anglesey flocked to hear him speak and to be baptised, and no doubt as his fame spread the Saint was inconveniently besieged by daily crowds of disciples. He had his humble dwelling by a well (in time, a Benedictine Priory was to be built here) but now Seiriol sought a more retired hermitage. Half a mile offshore there was a small island, and here he built himself another

cell to which he could retreat when he wished to meditate away from his followers. And so the island was given its first name of Priestholm by the Norse Christians of Anglesey. Later, after Seiriol's death, it was named Ynys Seiriol by the Welsh; and later still the swarms of puffins – which still come here – earned it the English name of Puffin Island.

Seiriol also had a chapel or hermitage on Penmaenmawr, 5 miles away beyond the shallows of what is now Conwy Bay. And the ancient record that tells of this seems to confirm what some geologists hold to be true: that there was once a tract of sea-marsh and sand between Puffin Island and the mainland of Wales. 'This Seiriol' (says the document) 'hadd an hermytage at Penmaen Mawr, and there hadd a chappell where hee did bestowe much of his tyme in prayers ... and made from Priestholm to Penmaen Mawr a pavement whereupon hee might walke drye from his church at Priestholm to his chappell at Penmaen Mawr, the vale beynge very low grownde and wette, which pave may bee discerned from Penmaen Mawr to Priestholm when the sea is cleere, if a man liste to goe in a bote to see iit.'

Of St Seiriol's other accomplishments there is little record. Perhaps, though, it ranks as a very great achievement to be remembered in place-name and story for 1400 years.

The Walk

Anglesey: St Seiriol's Well and Penmon Point

How to get there: Drive to Beaumaris on the island of Anglesey, go through the village and past the old castle. After about 1½ miles, turn right, signposted 'Penmon 2½ miles'. This winding lane brings you to another right-hand turn sign-posted to Penmon Point; follow this until you see the ruins of the old priory on your left.

Start point: just beyond the priory. Grid ref: SH630807.

Distance: 2mls (3km) there and back (plus a short diversion)

Map: OS Explorer 263

Grade: Easy walk on paths and lane.

The priory buildings are interesting and so is the huge dove-cote on the right; there are notices with a brief history of both. You can also visit the church, which has a 1,000-year-old Celtic stone cross in it – this used to stand in a field behind the church but was removed in 1977 to prevent further damage.

For the well, head towards the dovecote and, when you have passed the old gate posts, turn sharp left, sign-posted, onto a small path. Follow this through a stone doorway in a wall overgrown with ivy which brings you to St Seiriol's well. This is where the holy man used to baptise converted heathen; the foundations of his cell are to your left. Just

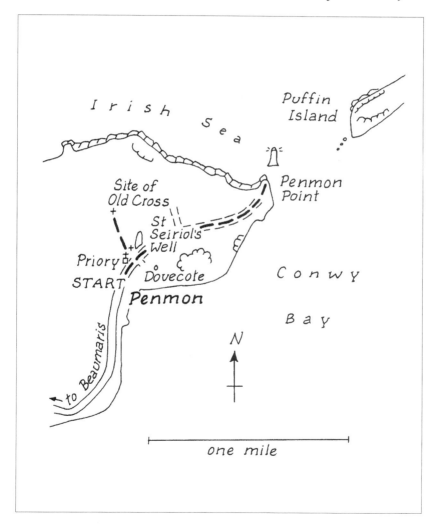

beyond the cell is an iron ladder-stile – if you cross this you can make the short pilgrimage (just over 0.5km, there and back) to the site of the old cross. Follow the path with a small limestone crag on your right. This soon joins a rutted track which turns uphill and, in a short distance, a small notice marks the site of the cross.

Retrace your steps back past the well to the lane, turn left uphill for an easy 15-minute walk to Penmon Point. The views here are tremendous – you can look back to the mountains of Snowdonia or just across the small, treacherous strait to Puffin Island, with its tower, where Seiriol built his hermitage. Penmaenmawr, where he had a second hermitage, can be seen far away to the right and we can assume that his causeway was between the two.

11. Llyn Idwal: The Lake that no Bird will Cross

In the year 1140, Owain, son of Cynan, was Prince of Gwynedd, a country corresponding to the modern Caernarfonshire and Merionethshire. Owain Gwynedd, as he was called, had nineteen sons, and one of them named Idwal was a very beautiful child. At the time when Idwal was a young boy, the Prince of Gwynedd was engaged in a fierce war with Howel, King of Powys. As there was a possibility that the forces of Powys would make a murderous foray into Gwynedd, Owain resolved to find some place of safety where Idwal could be hidden. At the same time, he wished to have the boy educated in the arts of poetry and the harp.

After seeking the advice, but to no avail, of his counsellors and friends he remembered a distant relative who lived in a small mansion in the midst of the craggy wilderness not far from St Curig's Chapel. Nefydd was this man's name, and Owain recalled that he was a bard and harpist of no common order. So young Idwal was sent as foster-son to Nefydd, to live and be instructed among the huge peaks that stand around Llyn Ogwen.

Now Nefydd was a very handsome man who had grown vainer with the years, so that he called himself Nefydd Hardd – Nefydd the Beautiful. He had a son of Idwal's age, named Dunawt. It was another of Nefydd's vanities to boast that Dunawt would grow up to be as beautiful as himself, though in fact Dunawt was a very plain youth and as dull in mind as he was homely in countenance. When he and Idwal sat together, as they often did while Nefydd gave them instruction, no one – not even a vain and wilfully blind father – could fail to see that Idwal was incomparably better-looking. And it was very quickly made clear to

Dunawt that his foster-brother was far cleverer than he could ever be.

As the days passed into weeks and the weeks into months, the envy and jealousy of both father and son smouldered more hotly until at last it burst into flame. Taking Dunawt aside, Nefydd suggested that he should lead Idwal into one of the wild mountain recesses to show him the lake that lay there beneath some of the grimmest precipices in Cambria.

"By its west shore the water is deep," he added. "If Prince Idwal were to fall in, Dunawt, he would drown, for neither he nor you are able to swim."

Dunawt was not so dull that he could understand what was proposed. He and Idwal set off up the mountainside and came to the big and gloomy lake between the precipices. They walked along the stony strand and then along the west shore, where smooth rocks overhung the water. A brutal thrust, a few moments of helpless agony, and the deed was done.

When the report of Idwal's death reached Owain Gwynedd he caused inquiry to be made, as a result of which it appeared certain that Idwal had been murdered at Nefydd's order. But the deed could not be proved against him. The Prince of Gwynedd then decreed that Nefydd and his posterity should be degraded from their rank of gentlemen and be bondsmen for ever.

As for the lake where his handsome son was drowned, it was called Llyn Idwal from that time forth, and because of the foul deed that was done there no bird will fly across its dark waters.

The Walk
Llyn Idwal

How to get there: The walk starts at the western end of Llyn Ogwen on the A5, from a small car park next to Ogwen Cottage Outdoor Centre.

Start point: car park, Ogwen Cottage. Grid ref: SH650603. If busy you can park at one of many lay-bys, which also avoids paying the National Park's rather large parking charge, and walk to the car park.

Distance: to the lake, there and back, 1¼ mls (2km); Idwal Slabs, 2½ mls (4km). Complete circuit approx. 5 mls (8km)

Map: OS Outdoor Leisure 17

Grade: Rough track, magnificent scenery. Allow 40 minutes for the short walk and up to 2½ hours for the longest walk.

In the car park are some toilets and a snack bar, to the left of these a track climbs up to the left, follow this over a stile and a wooden bridge. The broad, stony path mounts gently over open hillside, gradually entering the jaws of a great dent in the flanks of the Glyder range of mountains. In about half a mile you climb over another stile to stand near the end of the lake with Cwm Idwal's giant walls rising around you (1).

Nowhere in the British Isles can the heart of wild mountains be reached so easily. Llyn Idwal is popular with climbers, walkers and nature students but its many visitors do not spoil its grandeur. Y Garn towers above on the right, Glyder Fawr on the left. The line of cliffs above the farther end of lake is split by a giant cleft called the Devil's Kitchen. My

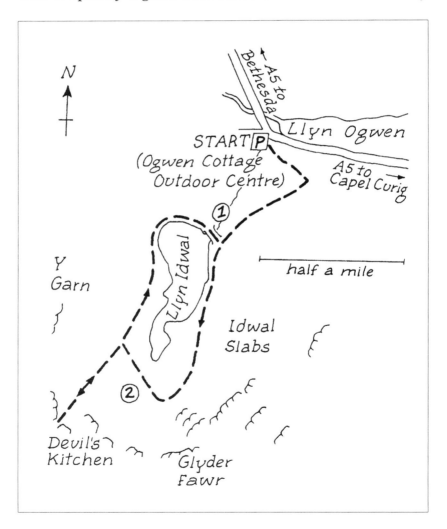

guess is that Dunawt administered the fatal push to Idwal over on your right where a grey wall of rock drops steeply into the lake. It is a good place to swim from or to sit and keep watch for any lake-crossing birds who haven't heard of the legend.

Extension 1: For the more energetic among you it is worth continuing your walk to the Idwal Slabs. Turn left along the lakeside path and follow this to an area of giant slabs on your left, on most good days you can sit and watch the rock climbers at play.

Extension 2: It is possible by continuing past these slabs and, by crossing a small river gorge (2), to go right around the lake with a small diversion to stand in the entrance to the Devil's Kitchen. **This part of the walk cannot be recommended for small children.**

12. Betws Garmon:
The Farmer who Caught a Fairy

The young farmer of Ystrad, the farm under the sheep-pastures of Moel Eilio, discovered where the fairy maidens used to dance on moonlit nights. It was a small field between the farmhouse and the river. One night he was in his usual hiding-place, watching them, when the most beautiful of them all danced very near to where he was hidden. He sprang out, caught her up in his arms, and ran with her to the house. With shrill cries of despair, the rest of the fairies vanished.

The captured fairy was well treated although she was firmly held prisoner, for the young farmer was deeply in love with her and wished her to marry him. But for all his protestations she would grant him nothing. At last, she told him that she would be his servant, but only if he could guess what her name was. He tried all the girls' names he could think of, but in vain. Then he thought of the dancing-place, and hid himself there once more. As he hoped, the fairy maidens were dancing that night, and talking together as they danced.

"If only she could be with us!" he heard one of them sigh. "But she is a prisoner of the humans. Alas, poor Penelope!"

If he had tried for a hundred years, the young farmer would never have guessed that name, but now he had it. Hurrying to the house; he greeted the fairy maiden triumphantly by her name, and once more asked her to marry him. Still she would not, though she now undertook to be his servant as she had agreed. With this he had to be content – and indeed there was soon no more contented farmer in all Gwynedd. Everything prospered for him and his fairy servant. The cows gave a full milking three times a day, the flocks and herds multiplied with magical speed, and in a

year he was farming (besides his own freehold of Ystrad) all the lands on the north side of Nant-y-Bettws to the top of Snowdon and all Cwrnbrwynog in Llanberis, a total extent of 5,000 acres.

Every night and morning the young farmer asked the fairy maiden to marry him. And at last she consented, with just one condition.

"You must never, never strike me with iron," she told him. "If that happens, I must leave you for ever and return to my own people."

He laughed at that strange condition, for such a blow could not pass between him and his true love. So they were married, and lived happily for several years. Then, one day, the young farmer went to the field to catch the pony, for he and his wife intended to ride to Caernarfon fair that day. The fairy wife went to help him. The pony was mischievous and would not come near the man who held the bridle and bit in his hand, and when the beast had played his tricks for a while the man lost his temper and hurled the bridle at him. It missed the pony and struck his wife.

The instant she felt the cold iron on her cheek she vanished. The last the husband knew of her was a wailing voice, very faint and growing fainter, imploring him to look after their children.

That was the end of the farmer's fairy marriage, but the children of the fairy Penelope grew up and had children of their own. The people of that valley had never been able to get their tongues round the fairy wife's strange name and turned Penelope into Pelling, and now her descendants were called Pellings. As long afterwards as the 19th century there were highly-respected Welsh folk who claimed fairy blood, and declared proudly that they were descended from the Pellings of Ystrad.

The Walk

Betws Garmon to the Meadows of Ystrad

How to get there: Betws Garmon is on the A4085 south-east from Caernarfon. Go through the village and look for the church.

Start point: near the small church on the right-hand side of the road if driving from Caernarfon. Grid ref: SH536576.

Distance: 1½ mls (2.4km)

Map: OS Outdoor Leisure 17

Grade: Easy paths across fields.

This is sheep country, so we advise leaving dogs at home. From the church, cross the road and go through a kissing gate next to the Bryn Gloch camp site, walk straight ahead next to a building then straight on along the campsite road. In a short distance you come to a 'T' junction, turn left here and walk down this road until you come to a toilet block. Turn right just before this, heading for a small wooden bridge over the river. If you look back from here, the small field where the fairies used to dance must have been between where you stand and what is now the road. If you look further back to the far hillside you can see the old farmhouse of Ystrad and, higher to its left, the open shafts of the disused mines, the opening of which no doubt chased the fairies away.

To continue your walk, cross the bridge and follow the public footpath signs to the right. Continue across the field towards a wire fence and turn left before you reach it, heading towards a gate and a small group of houses (1). Go through the houses to where the footpath signs point in several directions – your way lies to the left. From here, just follow the arrows and signs through various fields and gates until you eventually end on the embankment of the old Welsh Highland Railway (2). You can continue over the

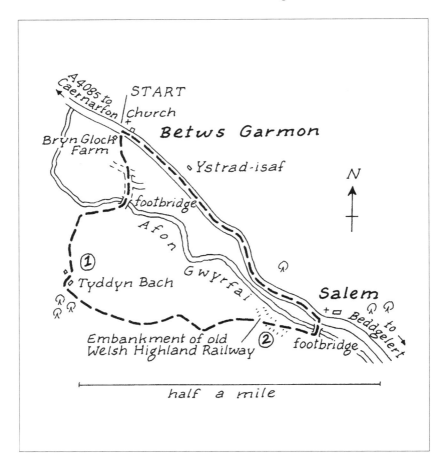

embankment towards the obvious footbridge over the river and return to your car by walking down the road. At the time of writing, it is possible to turn left at the railway embankment and follow it back over an old iron bridge and continue straight ahead until you reach the campsite from where you started. This variant was open at the time of writing but as there are plans to open the railway this may change sometime in the future – note that the route along the embankment is not a public right of way.

Lleyn and Tremadog Bay

13.
Borth y Gest: The Rising of the Lark

14.
Croesor: Helen's Spring

15.
Llithfaen: The Accursed Village

13. Borth y Gest:
The Rising of the Lark

In the year 1749, David Owen, a young and gifted 29-year-old Bard, lay dying. He called for his harp, saying that he had just heard one of the sweetest songs of heaven, and the harp was brought. In the short time before he died, the harpist played the famous tune Dafydd y Garreg Wen, 'David of the White Rock' to which, in later years, Sir Walter Scott added the English words. A less melancholy story is told of his earlier years, and concerns another of his famous compositions.

The name 'Borth-y-Gest' signifies 'the port of the land of Gest'; for the district westward along the coast from the mouth of the Glaslyn river was called Gest. In the 18th century, small coasting vessels plied to and from Borth-y-Gest, many of them hailing from France or Spain and carrying wines and silks, tobacco and spirits – cargoes that would show a very handsome profit if they could be sold without passing through the Customs. (Some of this contraband, it is said, found its way as far inland as Chirk, where it stocked the cellars of the great Sir Watkin Wynn.) In these days there lived at Borth-y-Gest a retired sea-captain named Captain Williams, who grew fat on the profit from the contraband trade and was always known as 'Captain Williams the Smuggler'. His house, Plas-y-Borth, was more like a tavern than a private house on most evenings, for he loved to hold a *noson lawen*, a 'merry evening', at which there would be music and dancing, and the wine and *cwrw da* (good ale) would flow freely. The heart and soul of the noson lawen was David Owen, the young harpist and composer of songs.

David's home was the farm Y Garreg Wen – the white rock – so named from the big pale-coloured rock that stood solitary on the hill just above it. The hill was between the farmhouses and the little port, and David was accustomed to walk that way on his visits to the Smuggler's house. One night in late spring, the noson lawen at Plas-y-Borth was over and David Owen was making his way back home by the familiar path over the hill. There had been song after song, and dance after dance, until the harpist's fingers were weary; but his skill had won him clamorous applause – and innumerable mugs of ale provided by his admirers. Indeed, his cargo of cwrw da impelled David to lie down and go to sleep, though he had reached the top of the hill and had only a few hundred yards to go to reach the farmhouse.

When he woke it was near sunrise of a May morning. He was lying on the dewy grass close to the side of the White Rock, with the distant mountains ranged against the glowing east. High above his head a lark, its wings tipped with golden light, was carrying its song far into the misty blue of the sky. In that moment of wonder David conceived the melody and words of 'Codiad yr Ehedydd', 'The Rising of the Lark', a song whose gaiety and tunefulness quickly made it popular through all Wales. You will still hear it sung at a noson lawen today. And it was adopted as the regimental march of the Welsh Guards.

The Walk

Borth y Gest to White Rock

How to get there: Borth y Gest, from where this walk starts is less than a mile from Porthmadog with delightful sandy coves just beyond the small bay, on a no-through road.

Start point: car park on the west side of the bay; Grid ref: SH565375.

Distance: Basic circular walk: 1¼ mls (2km). Can be extended to approx. 2½ mls (4km)

Map: OS Outdoor Leisure 18

Grade: Fairly short and easy. All right for small children, but some care needed on the steep path and beaches.

Though parts of this route are not shown as on public rights of way on the OS map, they are well used as a public amenity. Walk from the car park up the steep hill of Mersey Street towards the village school. Near the top, turn right with the school playground wall on your left. This lane turns sharp left behind the school and becomes a narrow path between bushes and then onto a bracken-covered hillside. Follow this path, taking time to look back for lovely views over the Maddock Estuary and the Moelwyn range of mountains.

When you pass through the remains of an old stone wall, a broad track curves round to your right. Follow this to a small lane with caravan emplacements. Turn left up this and in a few paces you will see a wooden stile in a wire fence on your right. Go over the stile and the White Rock comes into view on your left in a green field (1). There is a small tablet on the rock inscribed with the opening lines of David Owen's song – 'Cwyd, cwyd, ehedydd, cwyd'. The view from the rock is worth more than a quick glance and on a clear day you can see the Llyn Peninsula, the Rivals, Moel Hebog, Moel Du,

Lliwedd, the tip of Cnicht and the Moelwyns, the Maddock estuary with Harlech Castle beyond and Cadair Idris in the far distance.

Extension 1: To vary the return journey, try a longer way back. Go back over the stile and turn right on the small lane but walk only a few paces then turn sharp left between a few caravans in a small hollow. At the far end of the hollow there is a steep narrow path down between the thickets. Halfway

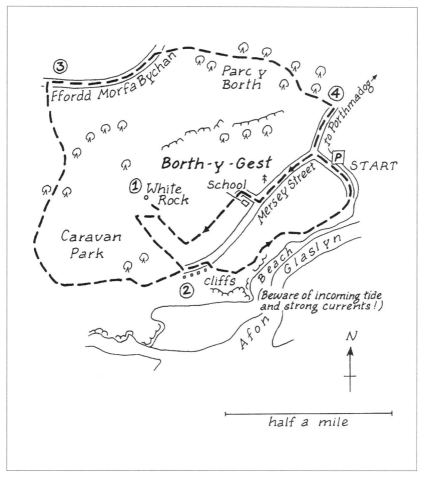

down, there is a junction, where you take the left-hand fork. Follow this until it emerges on a small lane with a row of cottages (2). Turn left, then in a short distance turn right down another path heading for the coast. Bear left when this forks and wander at leisure along the cliff tops back to Borth y Gest and your car. On this stretch there are many small coves some with steps down to them, a great place to stop a while and picnic or play on the beach with children.

Beware – the tide can fill these coves and cut you off and there can be strong currents running outside the rocks.

Extension 2: at point (2), rather than turning left, turn right and keep bearing right along the public footpaths around the caravan park until you reach the road (Ffordd Morfa Bychan). Turn right here (3) then right again just before a wooded area (Parc y Borth). Follow this path until you reach the path above the estuary (4) and turn right to return to your car.

14. Croesor: Helen's Spring

It is related that in the 4th century AD the Roman legions in Britain were commanded by Magnus Maximus, who in defence of Rome declared himself Emperor of Britain. In the Roman city of Segontium, where Caernarfon now stands, the Emperor Maximus wooed and won the beautiful Welsh princess Elen, afterwards known as Queen Helen of the Hosts because of her fondness for marching with her husband's legions. Helen was anxious that her countrymen throughout all Wales should be able to communicate freely with each other, and to this end she persuaded the Emperor to construct a paved road through the mountains from north to south of the country. Parts of that road were to endure for 1500 years, known to the Welsh as Sarn Elen, or Helen's Causeway; and it appears as Sarn Elen on the Ordnance Survey maps of today.

Queen Helen had two sons, both of whom grew up to hold command in the Emperor's army. Her favourite was the younger. One day Helen was journeying southward from Segontium with a large escort of legionaries, passing Llyn Cwellyn and marching thence through the Pass of Aberglaslyn in the direction of Ffestiniog. A separate body of soldiers followed some distance behind, as a rear-guard. This rearguard was commanded by Helen's younger son.

Beyond Aberglaslyn the Roman road climbed from Nantmor over the foot of Cnicht. Then, as now, it was a toilsome ascent, and when the Queen's party reached a spring a little way down on the other side Helen sat down to rest and drink the pure cold water. While she was still resting here, a breathless man came clattering down the stony trail, bringing tragic news from the rearguard.

What had happened was this: the track along the shore of Cwellyn lake passed below a grim crag called Castell Cidwm, where the giant Cidwm was reputed to live as in a fortress.

No sign of the giant had been seen by Helen and her escort, and they had journeyed on unmolested. But as the rearguard came beneath the frowning precipice an arrow – presumably shot by Cidwm – had sped down from the crags and killed Helen's favourite son.

There were many who whispered, afterwards, that it was the jealous elder brother who had shot the arrow, trusting that the fabled giant of the crag would be blamed. Perhaps Queen Helen herself suspected that this might be the terrible truth, for a great cry broke from her in her native tongue: "Croes awr – croes awr i mi!" ("Cursed hour – cursed hour to me!") And from this cry the spot took its name of Croesawr or Croesor; so that when – centuries later – a small village sprang up near Ffynnon Elen, as the spring was called, the name Croesor was transferred to the village. And both Croesor and Ffynnon Elen are there at the foot of Cnicht mountain, overlooking Traeth Mawr, to this day.

The Walk

Croesor and Ffynnon Elen

How to get there: from Porthmadog, take the A498 to Beddgelert but turn off on the B4410 two miles beyond Tremadog. This joins the A4085 at the village of Garreg. Turn left at the junction and look for a mediaeval-seeming archway on the right rather less than a quarter of a mile from the junction; at the time of writing there was no signpost to Croesor. Turn right at the arch and follow a charming lane for 2½ miles. If driving from Beddgelert, exit the village on the A498, turn left over Aberglaslyn bridge and left again when you reach the arch. As you enter the village, look for a sharp turn to the left and a car park sign.

Start point: small public car park next to river. Grid ref: SH632447.

Distance: Basic walk 1½ mls (2.5km). Longer walk 4½ mls (7km)

Map: OS Outdoor Leisure 18

Grade: Short and easy but worth extending for views.

Leave the car park and turn right, walking uphill towards the small chapel. Continue up the lane past the chapel until you reach a gate with a stony track beyond. Go through the gate and continue up the track, and after a few yards you will see on your right the animal drinking trough supplied from Ffynnon Elen. Just behind this is the sunken water tank put there when the old spring was diverted to make a water supply for Croesor village. 50 yards further on is another gate and just before you reach this, on your left in the wall, is the mossy mouth of the spring from which Queen Helen of the Hosts drank long ago (1).

In dry weather no water flows here now, as the diversion has sent the main flow of the spring underground and only after rain does the small mossy opening show itself as an active *ffynnon*.

You could return to your car from here, but the walk is well worth extending by continuing up the track. In five minutes you will emerge on a miniature pass with a grand view of Moel Hebog and the Nantle ridge with nearer, on your right, the heathery craigs of Yr Arddu. You could picnic here but it is better to carry on, ignoring a track to right which

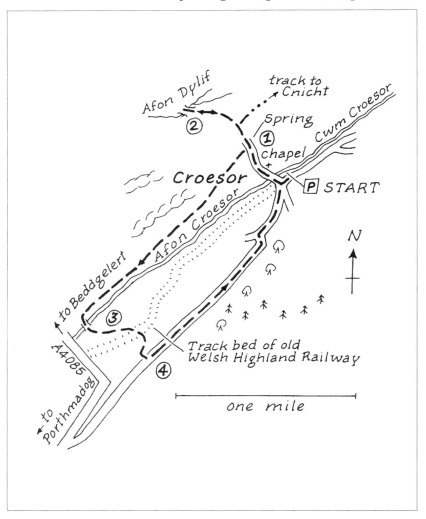

leads to Cnicht, and go on downhill, through another gate to an ideal picnic spot by the little river Dylif (2) where a bridge of huge stone slabs crosses the water.

Extension: The walk can be extended to approx 7km as follows: Return towards the village and, at point (1), head south-west along a footpath that soon runs alongside Afon Croesor. After 2km, just before a road, turn left (3) to soon cross the track of the previous Welsh Highland Railway and descend the hillside to a minor road (4), which you follow back to the village of Croesor. (To the north-east of the village, a tramway extension to the Welsh Highland Railway served the quarries of Croesor).

15. Llithfaen:
The Accursed Village

A very long time ago three holy men, barefooted monks from the neighbourhood of St Beuno's shrine, clambered down the craggy defile leading to Nant Gwrtheyrn, intending to preach the Christian gospel to the villagers in the remote hamlet at the sea's edge. Now the chief man of Nant Gwrtheyrn village was a pagan, and he would have none of the monk's gospel. Instead, he and his henchmen drove the three holy ones with stones and curses back up the glen to its precipitous rim. Then it was the turn of the monks for cursing, and each of them placed his own curse on the village at the foot of the glen. No one who was born in the village, cried one monk, should ever lie in consecrated ground after death. No male and female born therein should ever be able to marry each other, said another. And the third monk declared that the village of Nant Gwrtheyrn would decay and die, to become for ever a deserted ruin.

The years and the generations passed, and time showed that the first two of these curses, at least, were effective. The men of Nant Gwrtheyrn, who were mostly fishermen, died by drowning or by falling from the cliffs into deep water, and their bodies were not recovered. By similar chances the women, too, failed to achieve burial in the only consecrated ground in those parts, namely, St Beuno's churchyard at Clynnog. By now they were all Christians at Nant Gwrtheyrn, and the women – fearful of the curses – customarily left the village when they were of an age to marry; while the men sought their wives from places outside the valley.

There came a time, two or three hundred years ago, when a youth and a maiden who had both been born in the village resolved to defy the curse and marry. All went well at first.

The two exchanged presents on their wedding-morning (the bride's present to her man was a puppy-dog) and the sun shone brightly down through the branches of the ancient oaks which then grew near the village. The old tradition was followed – that the bride should feign bashfulness and hide herself, so that the bridegroom and his friends could seek her out and carry her off to the church. But when the groom's party came to look for the girl she was not to be found. They hallooed, they sought for hours. At nightfall she was still missing. Next day the distracted bridegroom and all the villagers sought high and low; and the next day and the next. But she was gone, never to be found. It was thought she had fallen from the cliffs into the sea, and was drowned, so that the curse should remain unbroken.

The poor bridegroom, broken-hearted and bereft of reason, paced every day up and down the shore with the dog, her wedding gift, in his arms. Month by month, year by year, he spent his time in this way, until the people of the village discovered that the dog he had carried about for so long was dead. They flung the body into the sea. And next day the man, too, was gone – drowned.

The years passed, but the tragic story was still remembered in Nant Gwrtheyrn. Then there came a night of terrible storm, with lightning smiting the cliffs above the village and rocks crashing down. A thunderbolt struck one of the old oaks near the village, splitting it open. In the morning, when the folk came to look at it, they saw that the tree had been hollow, and that a skeleton was gripped, as in a vice, by the narrow depths of that hollow trunk: a skeleton with long silky hair. They knew, then, where the bride in the old story had hidden herself.

The skeleton was placed reverently in a coffin, and a horse was harnessed to drag it up the precipitous ascent so that it could be taken to St Beuno's church for burial. But at the very top of the ascent, where the path ran along the cliff edge, the horse stumbled and fell down the precipice. The coffin was smashed into matchwood. And the bones of that skeleton were so scattered and lost among the boulders that there was no possibility of burial in ground consecrated or unconsecrated. Still the years passed. Roads and quarries brought new life to the north coast under the heights of Yr Eifl, and a thriving new village sprang up in Nant Gwrtheyrn. There were fine stone cottages, fertile gardens, a school, and a chapel. This became a happy community, fortunately situated and caring little for the old dark legends of centuries gone by. But what, then, of the third curse?

The Walk

Llithfaen and the Rivals

How to get there: Llithfaen, near to Nefyn and on the southern slopes of the Rivals (Yr Eifl), is your first objective for this walk. To reach it from Porthmadog follow the A497 through Criccieth and Llanystumdwy. One and a quarter miles after Llanystumdwy, turn right on the B4354 through Chwilog to Y Ffor where you keep straight on across the A499. Three miles further is a cross-roads where Llithfaen is signposted. Two and a half miles on this lane brings you to Llithfaen; keep straight on over the village cross-roads – uphill to where the lane emerges onto heathery slopes above the sea, half a mile beyond Llithfaen.

Start point: Continue along the lane to an obvious parking place on the left. Grid ref: SH353441; you cannot continue beyond here without permission.

Distance: basic walk 1½ mls (2.5km). Optional 3 to 4mls (5km to 6km) walk to Tre'r Ceiri hillfort on The Rivals.

Map: OS Explorer 254

Grade: Small lane but steep; 900ft to go down and to come up again. Optional walk in The Rivals is strenuous.

In the parking place there is a notice board with some information and alternative walks. Here you are 922ft above sea level. The highest peak of the Rivals, at 1949ft, rises above and you can just make out on its summit part of the iron age fort called Tre'r Ceiri, the town of giants. From the parking place, walk downhill through a gate. The lane continues through trees with drops on your right. Quite suddenly the view opens out and it is worth taking a small diversion at the bend in the road to look at the coastal cliffs, with Nant Gwrtheyrn below on your right. In 20 minutes you are down in the village. The chapel bears the date 1878 and in 1948 there was still a congregation here with children attending the village school, but then the quarrymen and their families left. Today it is a centre for Welsh learners and much restoration has taken place including a tea room in the Summer.

Although there is much debris and old quarry ruins around the deep glen, it is both scenic and charming – as is

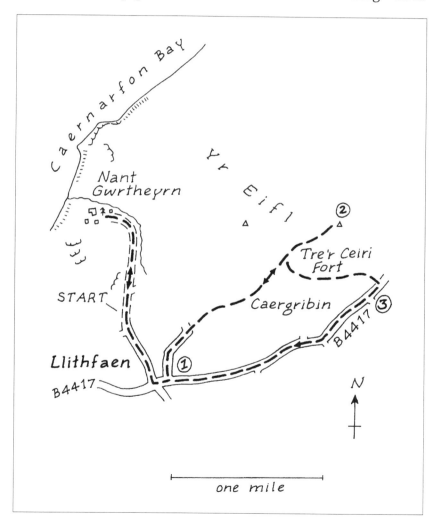

the beach – with good picnic spots. The return to your car is steep and will take about 40 minutes.

Optional Extra: a visit to this area would be incomplete without climbing at least one of the Rivals (Yr Eifl). You can easily complete a there-and-back visit directly from Llithfaen. Just a short distance along the B4417 in the direction of Llanaelhaearn, a minor road (1) runs first north and then bends to the north-west. The path then continues in the same direction, passing above Caergribin and arriving – after a climb of 280m (920ft) – at the spectacular Iron Age hillfort of Tre'r Ceiri (2). Substantial remains of the walls and ramparts can be seen.

Return either by retracing your steps or take the westerly route that winds down to pass between crumbling walls to arrive (3) at the B4417, where you pass through a kissing gate and turn right to return to Llithfaen.

Snowdon

16. Beddgelert:
The Story of Gelert

Llewelyn, the son of Iorwerth Drwyndwn, was a Prince of Wales in the 12th century, a man as renowned for his skill in battle as for his delight in hunting. In summer he would often reside with his family in a hunting lodge at the foot of Snowdon, near where the village of Beddgelert now stands. He had many dogs, but his favourite was Gelert, who was not only courageous in hunting the boar and the wolf but also a friend of the whole family – 'a lamb at home, a lion in the case'.

One day the Prince and his Princess went out hunting with their followers, leaving their baby son in the charge of a nurse and one servant. The nurse, as it turned out, was a scatterbrain unworthy of trust, for no sooner had her master and mistress ridden away to the sound of cheerful noises from the hunts-man's horn than she and the servant went off for a walk on the hills. The baby, son and heir to Prince Llewelyn, was left in his cradle, quite alone.

Meanwhile the hunt ranged far and wide, until it was noticed that Gelert was no longer among the dogs. The Prince was uneasy. Gelert was always foremost on the scent and first into the attack. Why had he abandoned the party – and where would he go, except back to the house? Llewelyn commanded an end to the chase and bade his followers return with him and his wife. They rode swiftly back and reached the hunting-lodge. And as they were dismounting, Gelert came running out of the house, covered with blood and wagging his tail.

The Princess, shrieking the name of her child, swooned away. Llewelyn rushed into the room where the baby had been – to find the cradle overturned, the bedclothes piled in a

bloodstained heap, and no sign of his infant son. It seemed to him that the dog must have killed the child. Blind with sorrow and fury, he drew his sword and drove it through poor Gelert, who gave a piercing yell as he died. Like a small echo, there came a shrill crying from beneath the cradle. One of the Prince's followers lifted the cradle, and there beneath it, quite unhurt, was the baby. Then Llewelyn pulled aside the pile of bedclothes, revealing the lifeless carcass of an enormous wolf, terrible even in death.

The Prince wept tears of remorse at this discovery. He owed his child's life to Gelert's keen instinct and courage, and he had rewarded the faithful dog with a fatal sword-stroke. Resolving that Gelert should be remembered as long as there were men and dogs on this earth, he caused the dog to be buried in a green meadow nearby, and the place marked with stones and shown to all who came.

A village sprang up in later years, and this was called Bedd Gelert, the Grave of Gelert. 800 years after Prince Llewelyn's over-hasty deed there may still be found, every year, a few visitors who, fulfil his wish:

> *'A pious monument I'll rear*
> *In memory of the brave;*
> *And passers-by will drop a tear*
> *On faithful Gelert's grave.'*

The Walk

Beddgelert: Gelert's Grave

How to get there: Beddgelert is at the junction of A4085 and A498, 4 miles south of Snowdon.

Start point: main car park in Beddgelert, close to the Royal Goat Hotel, where the A498 heads south from the village towards Porthmadog. Grid ref: SH588480.

Distance: from a few hundred metres to 3½ mls (5.6km)

Map: OS Outdoor Leisure 17

Grade: A short and easy 20 minutes or a moderate 3 hours if extended.

Leave the car park and turn left to walk down through the village. On reaching the point where the road crosses the old bridge over the River Colwyn, cross the road and continue down a small lane with the river on your left. At this point the old house on your right, now National Trust property, is the site of Prince Llewelyn's hunting lodge. Continue down the lane, past Gwynedd Crafts, to a footbridge over the River Glaslyn. Before you step onto the bridge, turn right through a small gate in the stone wall, there is a sign on the wall 'To Gelert's Grave'. Through the gate is a delightful path following the river downstream under trees. After 250 yards take the path on your right, beside a stone wall, leading directly to the grave of Gelert (1). Beneath a sycamore tree is a large slate slab inscribed with a brief version of the legend.

Modern research had discredited the story of Gelert and prefers the theory that the village is named for a saint or hermit called Kelert who was buried near here. However researches are quite often wrong and as you read the words carved on the slab you will probably find yourself deciding that this really is the grave of poor Gelert.

Extension: This very short walk is worth extending. Return as far as the small footbridge, cross this to the far side and turn right (2) along the bank of the Glaslyn. Continue following the path and then the track bed of the old Welsh Highland Railway through the Aberglaslyn pass – there are many picnic sites in this, the most picturesque pass in Wales. To follow the path right through the pass is more difficult than it used to be; due to a gross act of vandalism by the Ffestiniog Railway in placing gates across the old rail track just before the first of three tunnels. However, on reaching the first wooden gate you can drop down to the fisherman's path and scramble round a rock buttress to continue your walk – great care is needed with small children.

Follow the path until you exit onto a road at the old bridge (3) over the River Glaslyn, then turn right over the bridge and then left at the T-junction. Walk down the road for about 50 yards (beware of traffic on this section) and look for a path on your right which is ten yards before the entrance to Aberglaslyn Hall. This path is not very obvious, but is right next to the large road sign to Beddgelert. Take the path through woodland and cross a stile with a fence on your right. You soon come to a junction; take the path to the right and follow the obvious path up wooden steps. Cross a tiny bridge and follow the marker posts uphill. Climb steeply for about half an hour until you reach a stile over a high, drystone wall. Go over this and continue straight ahead. You have now left the woods and, in a few minutes, the path bears right to emerge on a great viewpoint above the Pass of Aberglaslyn (4). The view from here for the small gain in height is truly wonderful.

The path continues to a small tower and drops down to your left. You pass a stone structure and the path starts to drop back to the valley floor. This soon levels out and crosses open fields; it is a bit indistinct in places, so look for marker posts. The path exits on the edge of the village cemetery; go out of the iron gates (5) and turn left back to Beddgelert.

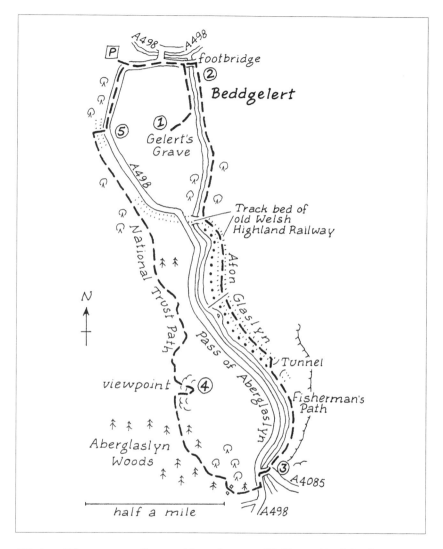

Note: *The route from Aberglasyn Hall to Beddgelert is a concessionary path provided by the National Trust. As such, it is not designated as a public right of way, and you will not find it on Ordnance Survey maps.*

17. Beddgelert:
Glyndŵr's Chimney

'Glyndwr's Chimney. 250ft.
First Ascent, Owain Glyndwr, circa 1400.'

This entry in the rock-climbing guidebook to Moel Hebog seems to confirm that the great Welsh leader, head of the rebellion against Henry IV of England, did the first recorded Welsh rock-climb. Here is how it happened.

Owen Glyndŵr (Glendower is the Anglicised form) was at the lowest ebb of his changing fortunes. His makeshift army was dispersed, his lands were in the possession of his enemies, and he himself was being hunted through Snowdonia by bands of King Henry's soldiers. Giving his pursuers the slip, he crossed the mountains into Nant Colwyn, and there found refuge in the house of an old friend named Rhys Goch – Red Rhys.

Hafod Garegog was the name of the house, and it stood in a lonely glen facing across the valley towards Moel Hebog, with no other dwelling near it. Before long, however, the news leaked out that a distinguished stranger was the guest of Red Rhys, and those who sought to kill or capture Owen Glyndŵr heard it. There came a day when a servant of Rhys Goch dashed up to Hafod Garegog to report that a large party of soldiers in light armour and carrying swords was approaching the house. Rhys and Owen swiftly dressed themselves in servants' clothing and made for the open mountainsides, Rhys heading for Nantmor and Owen running towards Aberglasglyn and the sea. But if they had hoped to puzzle the pursuers their hope was swiftly disappointed, for Owen was recognised at once and the men-at-arms concentrated on cutting off his escape.

The Welsh rebel leader then had no chance of using the

sea to win his way to freedom. He must turn for help to his native mountains. The wide semicircle of his hunters was almost within bowshot behind him as he clambered at top speed up the mountainside above the woods of Aberglaslyn. Close above frowned the line of precipices rimming the crest of Moel Hebog, the Hill of the Hawk, and Owen made for the left-hand end of these where a bald shoulder offered the only safe way over the mountain. Before he could reach it there was a hoarse, triumphant yell and he found his way barred by half-a-dozen soldiers. Desperate now, he made straight upward at the best of his failing speed, at last reaching the sloping walls of scree that buttressed the vertical crags overhead. The breathless shouts of his pursuers sounded close below him.

There was only once chance to escape now, and that an unlikely one: the vertical precipice was split by a cleft or chimney, nearly three hundred feet from top to bottom. If Owen could not get up it he was a dead man. He toiled up the scree with the hunt at his heels and launched himself at the steep rock. It gave Owen Glyndŵr safe hold for hand and foot, but none of the pursuing soldiers would dare an ascent where one slip meant death. While their quarry climbed on up the chimney, King Henry's men scrambled off to the left to gain the crest by an easier way. And when they reached it there was no sign of Owen, on the ridge or on the summit of Moel Hebog. Certain that he had fled downwards into Cwm Pennant on the farther side of the mountain, the soldiers hurried down and spent the rest of the day searching the valley.

They searched in vain. For Owen, after emerging at the top of his chimney, had run along the ridge to the verge of the northern precipice, Y Diffwys, and climbing down it a little way had hidden himself securely in a cave. And so the bold Welshman lived to fight another day.

The Walk

Beddgelert to Glyndŵr's escape

How to get there: Beddgelert is at the junction of A4085 and A498, 4 miles south of Snowdon.

Start point: main car park in Beddgelert, close to the Royal Goat Hotel, where the A498 heads south from the village towards Porthmadog. Grid ref: SH588480.

Distance: half a mile to 2 miles (1km to 3km). For a longer walk, see later!

Map: OS Outdoor Leisure 17

Grade: Easy walk of about 1 hour, fine views on a clear day.

Exit the car park and turn right, then take the lane to the right of the hotel that leads to a small housing estate. In a few yards this lane bears left but your way is to the right following the public footpath signs. A grassy track leads to a bridge over the old Welsh Highland railway line, which you cross and then go through a kissing gate. At this point you can see Moel Hebog directly above, the cliffs up which Owen Glendower escaped are those to the left of the highest point and a step in their skyline marks the top of Glendower's Chimney.

Beyond the gate, turn right between stone walls. The track leads, in a few minutes, to a small stream and a bridge to join a surfaced lane (1); if you turn right here you can be back at your car in 15 minutes. It is better, however, to turn left and follow the lane through a small pine wood. As you emerge from the wood, high above is the upper part of Y Diffwys where Owen hid in a cave after his chimney climb. Now the lane bends left round the farmhouse of Cwm Cloch Uchaf (2) and further up curls left past some farm buildings. From here the Moelwyn peaks come in sight ahead. Continue on the lane until it ends at a gate, then turn sharp left through another smaller gate (3) and head down a small grassy hill with fine views ahead and Beddgelert below in the trees. Go through a break in a stone wall and turn right, then follow the path to another stone wall with a gate. Go through this gate and turn left, keeping the wall on your left – the way can be boggy here. Follow the wall and the obvious path to end back

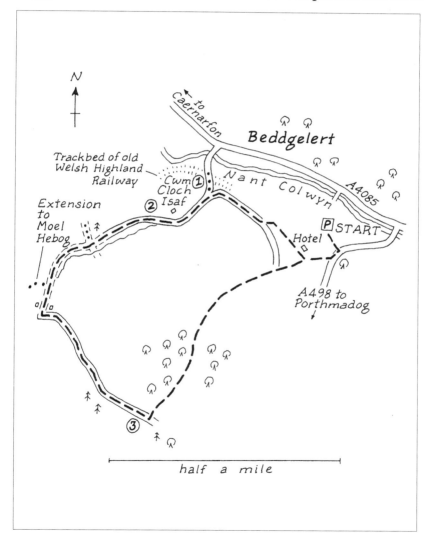

at the kissing gate and the railway bridge. Go over this and five minutes later, you are back at your car.

Extension 1: a popular excursion from Beddgelert is to ascend Moel Hebog (782 metres). Follow the walk description as far as point (2) to a junction of paths at Cwm Cloch (Grid reference SH545483). From here, a path leads just south of west to Moel Hebog for a there-and-back walk. This is only for the really fit!

Extension 2: this is a four-hour round trip to the cave of Owain Glyndŵr. Follow the route for Extension 1, as described above. Start by walking from here along the main route up Moel Hebog. But, after 100 yards, there is a gap in the wall on your right; cross to this, go through the gap and turn left. Keeping the wall on your left, follow this until you come to a drainage ditch, cross this at its easiest point and then head back to the wall. Follow it to a gate through this and ford a stream. Go over another stile to a path through some woodland from which you soon emerge on a forest track; turn left and follow this. The track joins another one but bear right, staying on the original track, and soon an open area appears on your right with fine views. Continue on until you reach a bridge, go over this to join another track, then turn left. You soon reach another junction and you turn left again.

You enter an area of older forest and cross a bridge. After about thirty paces there is another bridge. Here on your right, just before the second bridge, there is a track beside the stream. Take this and follow the small tumbling stream uphill – staying on its right bank and keeping the stream on your left. You come to an area of fallen trees and a subsidiary stream – a certain amount of care is needed here, especially with children, as you cross the stream and scramble past the trees. Rejoining the main stream, keep it on your left and eventually emerge on another forest track. Turn left for a few paces and then turn right over a bridge to follow the stream once more, now on its left bank. At the next forest track, again cross to the right bank of the stream and follow it through an area of felled trees, always keeping the friendly stream on your left. At the next forestry track, you can stop and, directly in front of you, is a cliff face with the cave of Owain Glyndŵr seen as a horizontal strip across its face close to the top. The view from here is magnificent and well worth the walk. The path does continue and for those with mountaineering experience, you can visit the cave but otherwise you should retrace your steps back to Beddgelert.

18. Snowdon:
King Arthur's Last Battle

The great days of the Round Table were over. Arthur and his knights had succeeded in driving the pagan Saxons back into England, and the mailed champions who had charged under the Red Dragon banner were dispersed. King Arthur himself was no longer young, and there were those, among them the treacherous Sir Modred, who whispered that it was time a new king ruled in Britain. Modred sent a message secretly to the leader of the Saxons, in eastern England, appointing a meeting-place in the mountains of North Wales. If the Saxon army would join him there, he said, he would raise a second army and together they would make an end of King Arthur and his power.

Arthur was in his place at Caerleon-upon-Usk when news of the renewed Saxon invasion was brought to him. Swiftly he gathered as many of his knights as he could find, including the faithful Sir Bedivere who had never left him, and marched northward. When he reached Dinas Emrys, a mile beyond Beddgelert up the Gwynant valley, a man of the valley told him that the great host of Saeson was encamped beneath the walls of the old city of Tregalan, in the upper part of Cwm Llan. So King Arthur and the remnant of his chivalry advanced up this deep valley that lies under the central summit of Snowdon.

The battle that followed lasted all that day. It was a winter's day, and from grey morning to grey evening the clash of steel and the battle-shout and the moans and screams of wounded men filled the wide cwm and echoed dismally from its crags. Hour by hour, foot by foot, the King's warriors forced their enemies farther into the cwm, and up the rocky hillside towards the crest of the precipice between Snowdon and Lliwedd. At nightfall the struggle had reached the crest. But it was a small and weary struggle now, for very few men were left alive: And here, in the gathering darkness of winter, King Arthur met his death.

Some say that a chance arrow slew Arthur, one of a last volley shot by the Saxons; and that Bwlch-y-Saethau, the Pass of the Arrows, was so called because of it. Others say that it was Modred himself that killed the King. Both, it seems, were sorely wounded when they met in the twilight on Bwlch-y-Saethau. Modred got in his blow first, and it was to be a deathblow. But Arthur lifted his own sword, Excalibur, and with one last great stroke clove through steel helmet, skull and brain. Modred fell. And Arthur, near to death, fell beside him.

Then Sir Bedivere carried him precariously down the crags to the shores of Llydaw, and there a black barge, wherein sat three beautiful women, waited. The dying King was borne away into the night mist, while such of his warriors as survived the battle made their way into a cave on the precipice-face of Lliwedd, there to await the second coming of the royal leader.

The Walk

A stroll in the foothills of Snowdon – or a climb to the summit

How to get there: drive to the top of the Llanberis Pass on the A4086, 6 miles from Llanberis and 5 miles from Capel Curig. From Beddgelert, the distance is 9 miles – follow the A498 and turn left at Pen-y-gwryd.

Start point: The Pen-y-Pass car park, Grid ref: SH628544. Get there early at holiday time or weekends because the cars of those starting out to climb Snowdon are parked here. If full, park at the bottom of the pass and catch a bus to the top.

Distance: 4½ mls (7km) round trip. Longer walk of 9 mls (14km).

Map: OS Outdoor Leisure 17

Grade: Basic walk is easy and suitable for small children in good weather – allow 2 hours. Allow all day for the ascent and descent of Snowdon!

The basic walk, on a broad track all the way, takes you as far into the heart of Snowdon as you can reasonably go without proper boots and clothing for mountains.

From the car park (near which there is a restaurant) follow the wide, gently climbing track across the mountainside. There are sure to be other people on it, for this is the Miners' Path that leads to the ascent of Snowdon by 'The Zigzags', above Glaslyn. The track gives a downward glimpse of the upper Gwynant valley before it curls round the flank on the right. Now it descends slightly past a small lake, Llyn Teyrn (1), beside which you see the ruins of the tiny houses where the men who worked the old copper-mines of Snowdon used to live, only going home at weekends. Beyond Llyn Teyrn it climbs again, still curving into the high glen walled by steep mountains that slowly opens ahead. When you come to Llyn Llydaw you see one of the grandest of all views of Snowdon

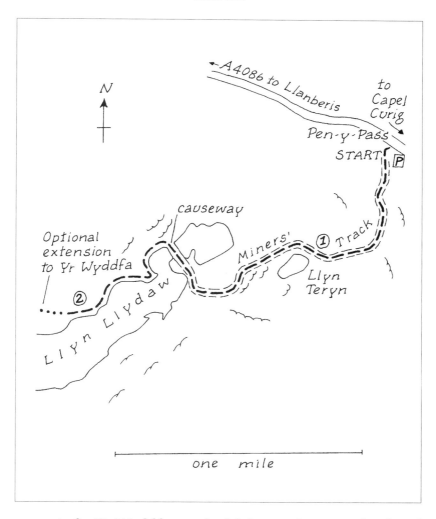

summit, for Yr Wyddfa – as the highest point in England and Wales is called – rises magnificently beyond the far end of the lake.

The track goes to the right, crossing an arm of the lake by a stone causeway. (In winter, or after very heavy rain, the causeway may be partly under water.) Follow the track round the lakeshore past the old copper mine and halt where it begins to climb steeply from the waterside (2). This is the terminus of the basic walk, for the return is made by the same route. And from here you can see the setting for the final acts of the King Arthur legend.

The huge precipice of Lliwedd looms opposite across the lake; its crest is 2,947ft above sea-level The lower crest to the right of it, separating it from the upsurge of Snowdon summit, is Bwlch-y-Saethau, the Pass of the Arrows, where the heathen hordes were driven back over the edge and where Arthur and Modred fought their last fight. It must have been by that precipitous way down the ridge to your right that Bedivere carried his dying master to the lake shore and the waiting barge, for the crags under Bwlch-y-Saethau are too steep for such work.

As for the last of the Round Table knights, they must have been good rock-climbers as well as stout fighters. The cave they are supposed to have entered is in the groove to the right of the central part of the precipice (hardly to be seen from below) and even a mountain goat would find it difficult to reach it from the crest where King Arthur's last battle was fought.

Extension: On a fine day, with a good weather forecast and suitable footwear and waterproofs, the more ambitious can safely continue all the way along the Miner's Track, passing the beautiful lake of Glaslyn and then climbing steeply up to join the track of the Snowdon Mountain Railway and – finally – Yr Wyddfa itself.

In season, and if the railway is operating, you can endure the ghastly café just below the summit if you are desperate for refreshment – and you can buy a postcard with a Snowdon postmark to prove that you made it to the top!

There are many alternative routes to the peak, but the easiest and safest return route is to go back the way you came.